I0790425

THE HOLY CRIP'S BIBLE

THE KIWE DON

authorHOUSE®

AuthorHouse™
1663 Liberty Drive
Bloomington, IN 47403
www.authorhouse.com
Phone: 833-262-8899

Published by AuthorHouse 01/17/2022

ISBN: 978-1-6655-1863-5 (sc)
ISBN: 978-1-6655-1862-8 (hc)
ISBN: 978-1-6655-1861-1 (e)

Library of Congress Control Number: 2021904522

Print information available on the last page.

CONTENTS

ACKNOWLEDGEMENTS

It is virtually impossible to appropriate acknowledgement venerations to a Nation so massive and potent with ride or die True Blues, we all know that nobody could salute us all, however it would be close to a transgression not to atleast name a few: First and foremost my cousin and mentors Harlem-Huc-a-Buc and Baby Bro "sex" violence "money and murder" was your invention as you and Bro took me and Lil Ice-Man to the Arlington double and said: "You gotta' touch'em!", To: Big Kato for hating "Ministers of Misinformation", to tha' Beast Money Marv forcing riders to ride or die. To: Askari, Tabari, Suma & Big Ant for adding the word "Consolidated" to my vocabulary. To Big Wiggles and down ass Papoose doing it the Broadway-way To: Chafu-Big Forehead for teaching me how to play dirty (lil Chafu), To: The Famous Underground Harlem connection, Treach and Evil, Truck and Bang. Wack and Ben-dog (my Ace) The Droopys, Evil and Ms. Lay-Lay, Black-Ed and Lil-CT. Harlems Finest Big Bob and The Watts, The Capone's and Docs, the Baby Boys and the Jakes, the Warlocs and Quakes, The Jim-bo's and Jimdog, the C-Rags and Frogs, The Baby Roc and the C-dogs Thumbs up to all our hogs, The Crip Roas, Big Peen and the Crip Toes. Ms. Tiny Mite, the Lee-Lees, Lil Bit, Peaches, Young Tiff and Ms. Virgin. That Rich Rolla' Coaster Neighborhood Understood connection from 1st Street to 190th its more than just a song. The Six pack's Finest: Big "Lil Man" and Tac, Mont and Greedy, Roscoe and Sad, 66 Brotherhood, Doc Thone, Lil Duck-Down, Lil Staccs, Q-Ric-Ric, C-Bone, Twin, Mad Dog (I miss you Pee-Pee), 89-Nugget, C-Dave, Casboo, 190 Frog & Cyco Mike, Young Brownie and the 118th Str Legends. That A-line from Big Kit and the Tag & Tray-girl sisters to lil Scooby on 116th. The Hub and a Dub connection, Watts up to the Days and Pygmies and the Phillips family, them who-riders Tuffy, Sporty and Spray Mike to them Baby Locs, my Spoony "G" dog Buddha & Holmes Street B-J Seven St., Fudge Town, P.J's Finest Tony Bogart and Sirpo, them young guns on Mona with the fat-cock-possee, Carver Park's Chico and Peaches, Southside Puncho and Brim, Santana Mike and Girch, N-hood Bay Rob Netty Bloce lil-C and Lou (my boy Cripta'nite), Mona Park and Original Front Heads got love, Crip Love! Long Beach Crip Tracy-Dee, Rob-Dog without my girl Ruthy, my boy Tee Fuller and fam that includes the Snoop Dog. My boy Ray Bone and Roc Head and Skinny, My Doves and LBC's Finest Reese Cup and Goldie Insane Baby Craft, Big C and Scatterbrain. Garden Bloce Shaka and C-bo, San Diego's Roc, Bay loc and Bullet. The last of a dying breed of Hoover Crips we love Hoova Lon, T-Ray, H-Sims, Hoova Hog, Big Bogart. Pasadena Raymond White Zeke (a true Crip if I ever saw one), Venice Shoreline Zig Zag, Tay Dog, Reps C-Capone, baby C-Nut, Killer and the feather stones, Terry Johnson-Tee Jay who introduced Teena Marie. 8-Tray Gangster Brown, Master Kody, Crazy-D, Diamond and Tracy 4-Tray Burt Train, Sunny, Bam Loo, 5-Tray Blue Shot Gun Crip's Sleepy, Bird Legs, Shiphead, The Pay Back Crips; Harbor City Crip's (Burglar), Riverside Crips, Main Street Mafia's Dale-Dog, Ice Mike, D-Loc, Droopy, Ms. Mo-Mo (Monique), and Doc-Rob.

The School Yard Crips, my boy Crazy Chris, Big Blue, Big Stupid, Swanny and Ms. Ray Ray, Big-40 oz, Ms.Gail and my young flesh Baby Snipe. To them Graveyard Crips D-loc, Satch-dog and Ken dog. My West Blvd. Crips Ronnie Tee, Ken-Bone, Tony-Tee, J-Stone and Blue. Them Geer gang Crips my cousin Smokey, T-Top and White-face Mike. Them Marvin Gangsters/Harlem Godfathers crippin the best in the deep West: Big Wicked, Big-Moe, Lil-Smiley, Baby Huey, Young Plot, etc... Them cold Playboy gangsters: Ms. Puppet, Poker, C-Boy, Nico and Ice Rat. Love to the trues from the newest Gateway Crips to the oldest Kitchen Crips off dat eastside: Mr. Lil-Smokey, Big Porky and Mouse. Front Street Watts Lefty-dog, Killer and Bozo, Back street Crips, All the Crips in the San Fernando Valley, the San Gabriel Valley, the Inland Empire, Orange County and Tustin, My Du rock Crips Ract-Tone, Mad-Will-rock, my Pomona Loc, Bugsy from Ghost Town, my Loc Shamu, and Gangsta Greg (Hey Crip Momma and Tasha) Sintown's Tray five Seven Crips, Santa Ana's sneek attack Watergate Crips, Comptons Crip projects: The Wilmington Arms and Park Village Samoan Crips, all over Island locos and them true Tungan Crips, All Asian Crips (T.R.G.'s) C-9000, Seven Trees Crips, all The loved ones throughout the other 47 states we inhabit, Crip love is full blast! World wide!

The Venerated Mad Circle

South Central L.A.'s Finest Rich Rollins 30's, 40's, 60's, 90's, 100's Rollin Strollin Controllin Snoop-Dogg, C-Dog, Baby Casper, Baby Cal, Peanut, Slip-Roc, Lil Fee, Big-U, Bandit, Baby Looney, Baby Crip-Cal my Nigz Lil Ripper, Lil Mad, Tad Pole, Speccs, Lil Shyster, Tiny Boo Boo and Tom Cat. XL's finest: The Snoops, The Snow Mans, The June Bugs and Spades, The Stoney's and Capones, T-Bone, Don Juan, the Budlettes and Forty Crips from the darkside, the parkside and the Ares. XC's Finest: Ms. Yo-Yo (92nd and Fig.) Space Ghost, Poppa Bird, Cujo, Smiley and Lil Donut, Scrouge. C's Finest: Ingle Watts 102 Raymond's Droopy's, Young Bam, Tank and Bang, 1^{e}11^{umz} Neighborhoods, Crowbar, Mando, Donut, Beercan, Big Pan, Monster, J-D (and Ice Cube's Lynchmob), W-C's (dub-Cee) Mad circle of blocc Crips, Keep C'walkin' to the Devil's dips at Southwest. 107 Bloccs Big Blacc, Eleven Tray (113th) Blocc. Ms. Zella, Bumper Jack, J-Bone, Rest in Peace Joker (my Lil Loc) Helen Keller Park's Finest, The Imperial Village, The Original Watergate Crips, The Brynhurst Players and K.O.D'S. XXX's Finest Harlem Booo, Big Den, Reece, Hawk, Lucifer, Joker, Rich, Juan, C-Rag, Baby C-Roc, Jimbo, Hilly Big Co-Co, Lil Booo, John John, D-Mac, Lil-Ali, Pokey, Tiki, Tiny Sponge, Tay-Tay, Crazy-O & Joker. Tear-drop, Jaekie Boy, El-Mac, Pop-Nose, Big Deevy, lil Tray, Earth Quake, Big Tim, Lefty, Big Doc.

Cuzzins Resting In Peace

"Far too many Trues to name, far tooo many fellow Crips to
blame, rivals to tame, gone tooo soon when these souls were slain,
yet we don't die we multiply again and again and again..."

A few notables...

Ms. Mecca, Ms. Co-Co, Ms. Crissy Loc, Ms. Jackie-girl, Hucabuc, Baby Bro, Hawk, Cadillac Jim, E-T, Fiddler Lil-Muggs, Lil Casper, Lil Mump (Poochie), Big Ken-Bone, Banker-T, Lil Looney, Scatter brain, Lil Insane, Rollin Forty Big Snoopy and Lil Pop-Eye, Nine owe-Nine ball, 1^{e}11um Slim and Big Killer. East Coast big Sike, Stoney, 59th T-Tiger, 69th Lil Smokey, Ms. Crip-Connie, Crip-Jackie 97th J-Box, Q-102 Lil Pee Pee 52 Broadway Angel, 52 Hoover Cadillac Bob and C-C (my dog Lil Boo), 107 Pookie, 8-Tray Lil Opie Marvin gangster Smiley, Play Boy Gangster Insane and Ghost. Venice Shoreline's Green Eyes. SYC's Blackie, Compton's Diamond Blue, Harlem-Big Dog and Mouse. Compton's Turtle and Baby Gangster. Watts Ms. Birdy-Jo, Benzo-AL, Tony Bogart, Philip Day, Harlem Silk and Lil PopNose, Hoovers Big Juda' Bean, 46st Hot Dog, Harlem Crip lil-Phil, Lil Ice Man and Lil Youngster...

The very 1st CRIP I saw buried
One Mister "Donald Ray" Winn B.K.A. Big
Sinbad-Original Brotherhood
Pamona's First Crip Community 1978 Farewell

The very finest Co-defendant I ever had
Stanley "Big Tookie" Williams
Sunrise: 12-29-1953   Sunset: 12-13-2005

All of the loved ones on Death row especially: Trech, Evil and Lil Fee

<u>Om Shanti</u>!

GENESIS

In the begining God, Jahova, Allah created the heavens and the earth. The earth was without form and void; and darkness was on the face of the deep. And the Spirit of God was hovering over the face of the waters. Then God said, "Let there be light"; and there was light. Divine text gives to man the knowledge and basic creations which ensued for five more glorious days until God took rest on the seventh day.

Today's world of science has arranged a sort of cosmic - Lunar calendar which suggests that each day represents thousands of millenniums starting of course with the "Big Bang". By choice the Crips find no conflict in reconciling the two, (although decent folks choose to war and massacre on these very grounds) because it remains the more reasonable still that Intelligent Design is the bedrock explanation. Evolution does not explain-away or justify how…"absolutely nothing" just simply became "absolutely something" therefore the Crips find that there is "absolutely" a Creator we simply call: "The Big Homie!" "Jahova", "God", "Allah", "our Lord and Savior" "Yaweh" or whatever name we're accustomed to using as it all boils down to the same fact that He's the Father/Creator who would've had to clap or snap His fingers even for there to be a Big Bang in the middle of nowhere.

So then… according to science, at 4.5 billion B.C.E. (Before Christ-or-Before the Common Era) the planet cooled off and formed. At 3 billion B.C.E. the first signs of primeval life stirs in the ocean in the form of Blue-green algae and bacteria. Then from 600 million to 4.4 million B.C.E. the 1st fossils are traced (discovered in Aramis, Ethiopia-1994). Then comes Australopithecus around 4.2 million down to 3.2 million B.C.E. followed by "Homo habilis" (handy man) at 2.5 million B.C.E. followed by "Homo erectus" (upright man) some of who head North leaving Africa around 1.7 million B.C.E. while those who remained became "Homo Sapien" around 100,000 B.C.E. then ultimately those travelers in the north (Caucas Mountains) became "Neanderthal" men and women around 70,000 B.C.E. losing their skin pigmentation and genuine empathy following a series of leprosy strains and albinism inbreedings. These Neanderthals with their beautiful reptilian-colored eyes continued North having a comfortable, high tolerance for the winter, widely spawned into "Cro-Magnons" 35,000-18,000 B.C.E. and crossed the Bering Straits into the Americas around 15,000 B.C.E. Meanwhile, in the old world below Homo Sapien-Sapiens began to develop settlements, cities and states as early as 10,000-4,000 B.C.E. There were glorious communal tribes saturating the entire continent of Africa all the way from the southern tip, to central Africa and the northern west coasts all the way to the historically touted, heavily recorded North: eastern regions where most of the earliest finds were unearthed. Finds that became the bookmark for what progresses and at what pace mankind was evolving. Finds such as the Egyptian calendar dated earliest at 4241 B.C.E., the Sumerian's earliest phonetic writings dated 3500 B.C.E., the various artifacts, tools and even metallurgy furnaces found all throughout the Sahara, Egypt, Ghana in the west, Sumeria in the east as well as North African Carthage (Spain) all confirmed these communities uses of copper between 3000-1000 B.C.E. as well as Bronze and had domesticated dogs, goats, sheep & horses.

The Crips being ecumenically wise and positioned all across the globe have learned to embrace layers and layers of truths that aren't so widely reported for the mainstream. Truths known by archeologist and renown paleontologist that determined homo habilis was the hunter-gatherers whom lived within the natural law of God and later came generations of homo erectus who transgressed the law. This may seem insignificant but this great shift by another name would be recognized as 'The Fall from Grace' or The Garden of Eden. If man weren't so arrogant as to just dismiss the possibility that all the other living creatures also communicate with their own kind and therefore would pass down their own version of the great fall of man, perhaps it would all start to make sense how the story of Adam and Eve came about. It would make great sense why, of all the living things, it is man who is said to be "cursed!". There is a law so then as Crips we believe we know it. The law is as natural as breathing: 'Eat and drink to live, don't just live to eat and drink'. 'Be a hunter and gather, even kill when you must, just survive by whatsoever means are necessary'. Necessary being the operative word in The Law. Man, just like insects, all creatures and animals of the land, sea and air must eat and must protect its life, this is absolutely necessary for all living things. Even the rose developed thorns as a defense mechanism within the law, it is not necessary for the rose to develop an ability to fire off or fling its thorns at distanced predators because the Law is structured around protecting and securing life, not in the taking and destroying of it. The Law, in a nutshell, promotes the Sanctity of Life so much so that once a ferocious pride of lions chase down and capture a zebra or antelope the remainder of the fleeing herd can stop running and are often found to resume their grazing within proximity of where the lions are devouring the kill. They instinctively know that the lions don't kill or hunt out of an emotional disdain for them and so, once they've secured a meal in respect for their own life, they [the lions] no longer pose the same threat. This is the Law that all living things once abided and were governed by.

Imagine the horror and utter disbelief that must have echoed throughout the land, sea and air when homo erectus first fell out with God, were driven from the fruitful garden of Eden and suddenly began to cover itself. It must've looked ridiculous and frightening to all the other creatures content with their own God-given coats. Then when Cain spilled the blood of his brother Abel (clearly) breaking the law as no imaginable necessity was at play. Creatures flying over head, lurking nearby or crawling under ground all knew that one particular creature had gone a foul of the law and so this creature was surely "cursed". This creature as homo erectus became known as Man and as the tales and this story (being passed down for thousands of years) found its way into heiroglyphs, phonetics and the spoken word its no wonder it is recorded and recalled as day one of the cursed era of man, the "Genesis" and simply the single most Greatest fork in the road where humans went one way while all of nature continued on in another direction. Perhaps when the egotistic modern man began to transcribe this legendary shift into books it was 'us' who then characterized this shift as the acquisition of wisdom and knowledge from the "Tree of Life" and suddenly we became as gods. The forbidden tree of good and evil being guarded by this ever so intelligent snake who enticed woman first and then it was she who seduced man causing the great rift between man and God. This even facilitating on some subliminal level that man was semi-blameless and otherwise noble were it not for woman. It is with these new eyes and cleaned glass windows we can look into a cage full of Apes and notice how the woman carries the burden of this past transgression. The story (so much older than homo sapien) was well known among all living things throughout the Paleolithic (Old Stone) age 2.5 million - 10,000 B.C.E., the Mesolithic (Middle Stone) age 8,000 B.C. and the Neolithic (New Stone) age 3,500 B.C.

By all accounts, the first world was destroyed by The Flood. In most religions in their perspective countries and in line with their cultures, the great flood certainly did occur, however the subsequent thereafter is where egotisms seemed to have entered their own takes about how the world starts again. In Mesopotamia for e.g. the surviving father is called "Utnapishtim" whom the Hebrews called "Noah". Then, the Mayans of Central America, they believed that "400 sons" survived by turning into fish; similarly the Babylonians believed that fish-like beings brought seeds of civilization (Oannes) which introduced writing, math, law and agriculture. The Greeks called the flood "Deucalion", so then... even as always, history is relative. Christianity, Islam, Judaism, even Satanist have come to accept the story of Noah's ark long before portions of it were unearthed by famous archeologists, therefore The Crip Cadre accepts it as true.

The Crips recognize that Noah had three sons; Shem, Ham and Japheth and Ham was the father of Canaan. Its always been a quietly guarded but easily confirmable fact that at least Ham was black as night and Egypt was as well. The Greek word Aigyptos or Aiguptos meant "black" which is where the name Egypt was derived from while its ancient inhabitants called themselves and their land "Kamit" or "Khemit", both meaning "Land of the blacks". Genesis 10:6-20. The Imperialistic European and American world uses the curse upon Ham as the explanation and exoneration their psychopathic racial behavior towards all blacks. Genesis 9:22-27 where Ham looked upon his father Noah's nakedness and thusly was cursed to be enslaved and father a race of slaves whom, generation after generation would serve the descendants of his brothers (who remarkably were white). An AWESOME-ALMIGHTY GOD curses a child and his seed for seeing his excessively drunk father but saw no fault in the inebriated adult who exposes himself? sounds perfectly white, perfectly Euro-Imperialistic and indeed perfectly arbitrary as the laws are today. So this false hood has no place in the hearts, minds and souls of any Crip of any race.

A few hundred years later, aprx. 2100 B.C. Abram (B.K.A. Abraham) is born in "Ur" a city of Sumera in Southern Mesopotamia (Iraq) then migrated to Canaan. Following the great dispersing/scattering of all the people for attempting to build the tower of Babel, each people had to go their separate ways, settle their own new lands and communicate in their own esoteric languages which most likely would imply the beginning of all these new races. However, the next man chosen to father another nation was aesthetically tied to the blacks. Abram was 99 yrs. old when The Lord finally changed his name to be Abraham - father of many nations around 2000 B.C. His wife Sarah being true to the game recognized that she couldn't get pregnant and so she sent her own young slave-girl in (Egyptian maidservant named Hagar) to whom which bore a son named Ishmael for Abram in order that the covenant might be manifested but God being God said "No!" and blessed Sarah at 90 yrs. old to bring forth a son whom they named Isaac as God had commanded.

Almost all of the major religions agree to these times and this era even as archaeologist have found evidences that support these accounts so then... after much debate this is a set of true recordings which is faithfully accepted and adopted by the Crip Cadre.

The story of Sodom and Gomorrah rings true for Greek mythology; Roman poet Ovid describes it as: Jupiter and Mercury comes down disguised as mortal men to visit the city "Phrygia" (now - Central Turkey) so then when they were treated so cruel, destroyed the city but spared only the one elderly couple whom had housed them. (Greeks being well-known acceptors of homosexuality). Meanwhile they construe the tale of the salt pillar as the musician Orpheus' wife Eurydice. Others believe that Israel created the story emphasizing Lot's daughters having to get themselves pregnant by their dad as the explanation for the births of their enemies, the Moabites and the Ammonites, nevertheless, archaeologist studying this early bronz era have said that the region was in fact checkered with oil deposits any of which was equal to a powder-keg just below a sand castle, i.e. these two cities really did go up in flames! To this day, all that remains is the Dead Sea as well as a few salt pillars therefore The Crips believe its TRUE!!! Nothing else explains how such a well-watered, fertile area could become a virtual wasteland with even the sea itself being filled with salt pillars and brimstones just as if they'd rained down from the heavens. This is the only sexual act we find as taboo and that is the art of male homosexuality, the very act which got its name from this city of men, this ruined city once called Sodom, (i.e. sodomizing another man isn't Crip like) therefore in order to maintain our strong cities, feminizing a loc is forbidden. Those who are born of this nature, we still can regard but you're just not Crip material.

Our predatorial gladiator brawls in the jail and prison cells shall no longer be crowned/rewarded with the manhood of our defeated adversary nor lost to a stronger Crip Dog. The oldest set of laws were those delivered through Abraham and Moses aprx. 2000 B.C. for the 12 tribes of Israel. These Children of Israel have been redefined through the years and somehow cast as the Jewish people particularly whom have maintained a significant amount of Neanderthal blood to appear as white. These laws have become the exclusive religion known as Judaism, the covenant between God and his "chosen people". Meanwhile aprx. 1500 B.C. (just off to the east) Hinduism is the African-Indian practice among a people only mildly mixed with Neanderthal, just barely enough to influence their hair growth patterns. Further east is Taoism and in Japan Shintoism came around the 6th Century B.C. exactly around the time when the Persian empire had introduced their prophet Zoroaster who, unlike the religions on their east consumed with yin-yang and the integral behaviors, he taught that people are of good or evil, they are living in the darkness or the light. All of this history tells the Crips today is the day, it tells us that Today's era is that Great Future Tomorrow that yesterday's world of people knew would One day come...We are here! We are greater than all the tribes of Israel, we are bolder than the Persian and Roman armies, we are more innovative than the Egyptians, Assyrians and the Greeks. We can be more compassionate than the Nubians that softly conquered Egypt aprx. 750 B.C. or as diabolical as the Carthagenians under Hannibal's command as they shook Rome to its core with panic and fear. We are the Royal Blue National Flag bearers who simply refuse to die.

In order for us as Crips to settle our minds of steel and hearts of stone upon a way of life, our foundation has to be settled absolutely on the Truth. This means more than just the memorizing of his storied history as taught to us but the unbiased evaluation of how and why everything played out the way that it did for both sides in His Story and all of ours. The Truth is... all human existence began in tribes and communities the way we are today. The truth is... within all tribes and communities there were disputes internally and externally with other neighboring tribes and/or communities however, NEVER was there EVER any mass murders or fields of bodies and body parts strewn all over the place until the Neanderthal inspired totalitarianisms seeped in. It was much more than everyone just learning that we could just club a woman over the head and drag her home then put her to work, it morphed into an agricultural revolution and structural control that allowed one tribe to be predators toward another and in a sense, club that weaker tribe or smaller community over the head, drag them and/or their possessions home (as spoils) then put them all to work. This callous creativity is often played down or is touted as the positive revolutionizing of humans ability to survive tough seasons and thrive. Instead of having to hunt hard and eat modestly, man can now sit on a throne or in his home and live off of the fruits of someone elses labors. The cause and effects of this shift in human behavior can be matched by no other. This is the catapult for wars as people and as tribes and communities all had to fight and defend their domains. This was of course the catapult for classisms and race-isms, for weapons and walls then ultimately deceptions and laws. This behavior coupled with Capitalism ignited greed so that suddenly the cycle of nature could no longer keep up! Whole herds of livestock, whole schools of fish, whole fields of fruits and vegetables all wiped out and/or stored up by one man destined or so determined to sell it or watch it expire (only to throw it away) rather than see it consumed by some hungry person for free. All of these symptoms of the so-called agriculture revolution snow balled into even bigger, more sinister evolutions. Weapons and wars developed from common hunting tools such as sharpened rock-tipped spears and arrows to the smeltings in the bronze & iron age for swords and shields and armor, the catapulting of flaming projectiles over a city's protective wall, then giant armies, ships, cannons and guns just kept this snowball rolling even faster. Once it congealed with the snowball of deceptions and laws it became a devastating

Emperialistic super snowball, it just couldn't be denied because now all its victims are merely criminals, transgressors, infidels, scumbags, towel heads, illegal aliens, refugees, thugs, fugitives from justice, cockroaches, chinks, commies, jew-boys, spicks, niggers, gypsies, etc... even as it keeps on rolling to this day simultaneously annihilating and deceiving more than ever before but the holy Crip Scriptures don't share the same appetite so we are not so easily deceived. We're of the old Original laws that nature depended on. All we want and need is what it takes to keep us and our loved ones alive, the Crips mean to survive!

It is precisely those intentions to survive that define us, the C-nation. It is our stalwart endeavor to exist by the True Laws of Nature (designed and perfectly balanced by God) to where no species would become endangered, to where everybody has the means to survive by showing and proving that they are the fittest. Yet its this method of living that they call madness because its out of step with Empirialism protocols of slaving and begging and studying and praying to be selected to hold this luxurious office or job or lucrative livelihood dangling in front of as: "The American dream"! We are called monsters and failures by those fortunate few who were selected because they suddenly believe that any one and everyone willing to do all the hard work and butt kissing that they did can then also be selected and can have the American dream, however, The Crips have done the math so we know that the bulk of us are destined to serve the empire no matter what and so we choose to follow the nature of all of Gods other living things, we "go get ours" and we refuse to beg or crawl, we roar and hunt like the lion, we lie in waite like the panther, we patrol and sniff like the shark, the eagle and the wolves, we commune together, we push, pull and strive and yes, we Rise!!! The most deplorable and sinister actions taken by humans, the most dishonorable type of character anyone could practice is the justifying of injustices and this is actually the bedrock function of that menacing snowball of deceptions and laws that America calls the media and government. Now it should be clear to you why we chant "Death before Dishonor" and we practice it so defiantly. What kind of society has people starving while leaning against the wall of the local grocery store? What kind of people tolerate the homelessness of men, women and children on the same boardwalks and boulevards where hotels, apartments and motels all sit, holding empty rooms for patrons only, furthermore...

what kind of Justices so eagerly jail any of these men, women and children for daring to correct their unfortunate situations despite their lack of currency papers, plastics and coins? God told them to have but the will and even like the pigeon or junk yard dog "Go get yours!" and survive by any means necessary! There was no money in the Garden of Eden, no supermarkets for the countless creatures of the land, sea and air and yet they all survive and by God so shall we!!!

Vis medicatrix naturae (pronounced: wēes-me-di'käh-triks-näh'tōō-rī) [Latin]=The healing power of nature.

Survival becomes the paramount task that a people, a community or a civilization can face. This lesson we learned from our elders, the ancient Egyptians, who were so welcoming and far too hospitable to all the white and yellow foreigners from the north that claimed themselves to be humbled visitors and ambassadors of peace but waited patiently for their moment, that one brief moment in time where a people relaxes their personal mission to survive the threats of the outside world and chooses rather to focus inward on the minuscule issues within their own collective because it is then that the golden rule of war echoes..."together we stand, divided we fall!", and so, it was at such a moment that such a mistake cost the greatest civilization such as the Egyptians such a fall from grace and only by learning and sticking to the Holy script such as this shall we avoid the path that leads to repeating this history.

The earliest records on these magnificent Africans begins rightly with the Thinite dynasty 3200-2780 B.C. Egypt's first and second dynasties where black people called themselves TA-Merrians or people of Khemit. This was the development era for the precious metals, fine arts & regulating the Nile. Djoser (or Zoser) often called the "Architectual lover", He employed and exalted (as builder of the famous step-pyramid) a genius named Imhotep. (The Greeks called him Aesculapius) as Imhotep also fathered medicine, invented the caduceus (The staff with wings and entwined by two snakes = a medical symbol) and Imhotep was later Diefied as the great god of medicine aprx. 1500 yrs. before Hypocrates of Greece is born. Pharaoh Djoser ruled as the Memphite dynasty aprx. 2780-2270, the 3rd, 4th and 6th dynasty because the 5th dynasty in between his reign was a predominate era of religion ruled by the Sun-god "RA". Ironically this was actually the most "creative" era completing a litany of works such as: "Treatise on philosophical maxims", The pyramid "Unas" at Sakhara which contained the "1st pyramid text", the book of the "coming forth by day" (Egyptian Book of the dead), many disciplines in social and physical science, architecture, Religion, Philosophy, fine arts, jewelry and literature. "Ra" was added to many pharaohs names thereafter. 2270-2100 The seventh-thru-the tenth dynasty experienced a great deal of political disorder due to the large influx of Asian foreigners requiring laws that encouraged and regulated the marriages and high social status for the off spring. Also the transfer of powers to the Courts after Pepi II reign ended. 2100-1675 The eleventh-thru-the fourteenth dynasty marks the "Middle Kingdom" period. This was the most devastating period at that time in history but is also the most educational for us here in the present. We are the future they so desperately wished they could imagine and lessons of this "The Middle Kingdom Mentality" shall navigate us Excellently toward the future that we now so desperately wish we could accurately imagine and visualize. Learning from history and the critical mistakes our ancestors made shall give us hope against repeating them. "The Middle Kingdom period was a time of chaos and family wars between minor kings, between lords of Ahnasis and Hemonthis (Arab-Armant) lords. Pharaoh Mentu-hotep's dynasty refounded authoritative power along with the Supreme Luxor [Thebes according to Greeks & Romans] and the sceptre of the most glorious Son of the Sun Pharaoh Amen-em-hat I who immediately called for the worship of Amen as official religion. (Amen is still used to end prayer or in worship = Yes!). Amen-em-hat IV and one of the few Queen-Pharaohs to rule Egypt, Queen Skemiophris followed by the feisty Sebek-hoteps (The Dwarf Kings) all fell short in maintaining the illustrious security standards of predecessors Amen-em-hat I and II so they lost to the Hyksos Asians. These Semitics were the 1st non-Africans to rule Egypt (1676-1675 B.C.E.) 1600-1555 B.C.E. The XVIth Dynasty African spirits of revolt began to mount against the Semitic Asians rule, directed by three Luxor Pharaohs Sequen-en-Ra I and II plus Seqen-en-Ra III died still clutching his weapon from the battle. Finally the third son Pharaoh Amhose I achieves victory driving the Hyksos out of Egypt even chasing them as far as Palestine (now partly Israel) ending this era. 1555-1090 B.C.E. The XVIIth-XIXth Dynasty is known as "The New Kingdom" period where the Pharaoh Neb-pehti-Ra-Ashmes (a.k.a.

Amasis) founded a mighty dynasty that ruled for over 200 years, Buried in the Luxor region which other rulers named the: "Dira-abu-N-Naga" (or Naga), his mummy still resides there at the museum in Cairo. His sons Amen-hotep I and II both lived, ruled and died quietly but their successor Amen-hotep III managed the great installment of the "Correspondence of Tell-el-Amarna" to better deal with the marriages between African Ta-Merrians and the Asian Semites from Babylon intending to cement their political and economic status; this new installment required the total surrender of all military control to the Pharaoh this time making it a great security installment. This is a method still practiced by the Crip Cadre even today (albeit unconsciously) as all the nearby taggers, rappers, hustlers, dancers, pimps, players and activist all concede to authority before persuing our women. 1515 B.C.E. The New Kingdom period is anointed by its 1st woman The Queen-King Pharaoh Hatshep-sut who ruled gloriously and even traced her lineage back to an alleged sexual encounter between her mother and the gods. (The hieroglyphics mostly destroyed). 1361-1352 B.C.E. The XVIIIth Dynasty is marked by one of the most recognized names of all the Egyptian Pharaohs King Tut-Ankh-Amen (or King Tut) who himself was not a direct successor to the Throne but got there through Amen-hotep IV's eldest of seven daughters whom he married after his 9th birthday (born aprx. 1370, took the throne 1361-1352 B.C.E.), his reign lasted another 9 years and nine is still one of our holy numbers today. The King Tut-Ankh-Amen name is a continued homage to "Amen" but also the Egyptian cross-like symbol that means "Eternal Life" and/or "For Eternity" is called an "Ankh" if it has a loop as its upper verticle arm. (1300 yrs. before crucifixion). 1340-1200 B.C.E. The XIXth Dynasty Pharaohs Her-em-heb (then a very old Rameses I) was so old he shared the throne with his only son Seti I who conquered Palestine before it was ultimately settled by the Haribus (Hebrews, Jews and Israelites). After Seti I (also called Sethos I) ruled over 20 yrs. Ramese II (son of Seti I) had 13 sons. Pharaohs Meneptah reigned and immediately led Egypt (Ta-Merry) to war with Lebu (Libya) and Palestine according to the accounts in his famous "Israel Stele" inscriptions however, his father Rameses II made his significant claim to fame through Bible records with Moses wanting freedom for the slaves, ultimately the "Exodus" out of Egypt led the children of Israel to conquer several small kingdoms throughout Asia-minor known today as Israel and the Middle East.

1200-1085 B.C.E. The XXth Dynasty Rameses IIIrd through IXth were known as the Rameside Kings (none of these Rameses were related to Rameses I and II). The reign of these seven Rameses passed within 21 yrs and very little record survived as this was the worst period since the New Kingdom period began. Chaos and horror took over in the communities, looting of the tombs and pyramids were widespread until the Rameside period finally ended.

1085-718 B.C.E. The XXIst-XXIIIrd Dynasty was the Tanite and Bubasite period during which time most dark skinned people were divided in the fued between Rehoboan of southern Palestine and Jeroboan of North Palestine and it wasn't their war. Finally Libyan Chief (also recorded in Books of Moses) ruled from 916-936 after King Solomon of Palestine passed so Shishak established "Law and Order".

718-525 B.C.E. The XXIVth - XXVth Dynasty was the Saite and Ethiopian periods where calm had returned.

525-332 B.C.E. The XXVIIIth - XXXIst Dynasty was the Old Persian and Mendesian periods where dark skinned Egyptians migrated and/or fled (404-394 The Tusi and Twa-Bahutu often called Pygmies and Watusis) out of Egypt in mass 378-341. The XXXth dynasty was ruled by Pharaoh Nectanebus I, the last pure African King then came 332-30 B.C.E. The "Greek Epoch era", followed by the Ptolemaic period (Ptolemy I thru XVth) including the Cleopatras whom ruled as VIth and VIIIth who was the daughter of Ptelemy VIIIth. Then came the "Post Dynastic period" dark times 30 B.C.E. The XXXIIIrd which saw the Birth, Death, Burial and Resurrection of Jesus Christ (aprx. 6 B.C.E. - 30 A.D.) as well as Royal family betrayals, murders, suicide, infanticide (Killing infants) wars and general destruction until 640. A.D where those who wanted peace melted back down into their own community tribes in the forests and mountains. Of course now, to know this history puts you on guard not to repeat it. The skin-tone of the Egyptians of today is just as phony as was those prayers and promises of the barbarian and warmongers that 1st came in singing Peace. It is no wonder that the Greatest and the Great historians have always been put out, put to death or put in line regarding what they say. Thousands and thousands of tribes throughout the Mother

Continent Africa all suffered the annihilations of their elder-historians and all their parchments which told their history, their stories, even along the Nile where Neanderthal behavior pillaged the library in Alexandria, (the great College and learning capitol of the world) but thankfully because bits of greed prevailed, significant slivers of intellectual property survived even though only to be claimed as Greek thought and brilliances, those slivers were informationals that the world couldn't progress without.

So then... Herodotus (485-425 B.C.E. aprx.) suddenly became known as Europes 1st historian (a Greek) who himself challenged the world to recognize that morality and ethics are relative to each people's particular culture. He wisely used a story where the Persian King Darius calls Greeks into his presence, offers them riches to eat the bodies of their dead fathers but the Greeks were repulsed and said "for no sum would we defile our dead [fathers]!". The king then called in the tribe Callatians who view it as honorable to eat their dead but then offered them riches only to burn the bodies of their dead fathers and immediately they were repulsed and swore "for no sum would we defile our dead fathers!". Culturally one people finds honor in the flames while the other one finds honor in consuming their loved ones so that Herodotus declared..."Culture is King!". He explored the ethics and morals of war (with the mighty Persians) as well then came Socrates (470-398 B.C.E. aprx.) who contributed so much to the conversations of Justice, Morality and even God, before he was condemned to death in Athens 398 B.C.E. yet his pupil lived on. Socrates put forth philosophical questions about Justice, morality and religion which boggled the human mind even still today. One famous Socratic paradox infers that "no one is willingly bad" but that "people do wrong because they have not the knowledge (circumstantial mentality) to do right". I believe another was this dialectic on Religion which his pupil Plato would later respond to:

Is God willing to prevent evil but not able, then He is not Omnipotent

Is He able but not willing, then He is malevolent

Is He both willing and able, then whence cometh evil

Is He neither able nor willing, then why call Him God?

-Socrates

If I choose to believe that there is a god and then there is no god, I have lost nothing.

If I choose not to believe there is a god and alas there is a God, surely I have lost everything...

-Plato

Plato (428-348) is widely considered to be the greatest philosopher ever. In his most famous work "The Republic" he[11] describes a perfect society where justice reigns because (and when) the people love justice and not because they fear the consequences of doing evil. It also spurred into existence the movement called "Ethical Egotism" a moral doctrine which says we should strive to maximize our own individual self interests positively. 385 B.C.E. Plato begins his Academy in Athens. Philip II becomes King of Macedon and hires (343 B.C.E.) young study of Plato's Academy to tutor his 13 yr. old son named Alexander, the tutor's name: Aristotle (384-322 B.C.E.) after King Philip's empire consumes all of the Athenians and Thebans he is assassinated leaving his well-schooled son to become "Alexander The Great" who finally conquers Persian Empire (The then Greatest Empire since the Egyptian Dynastic period) and Greece, City Alexandria is founded aprx. 326 B.C.E. Aristotle much like Socrates and Plato ignites ethical & moral reasoning that shapes Western civilization even turning "Logic" into a science still being studied in College today. In short, the Aristotelian Principal (one of his most famous) believes that a person's good is mainly determined by what rational plan of life a person chooses deliberatively from the maximal class of plans. That a person's self-respect (or self-esteem) is grounded in his or her sense of self value and his secure conviction that his concepts of good (and Crip-honor) are right making his plan really worth carrying out. Also self-respect implies a confidence in our own ability and power to fulfill our intentions, not

---

[1] [1] The Ring of Gyges - a scene from Plato's Republic where he uses a fictional dialogue between Socrates vs. Glaucon is to our morals if we held the ring that creates invisibility and therewith opportunity with absolute impunity.

being so plagued by failure and self-doubt that our endeavors become as impossibilities and goals not really worth us giving our hearts and souls to accomplish.

This is the "anti-snitch" philosophy, it is a fact that people snitch in every organization ranging from the military to the mafias and militias. People who once seemed committed to a cause will suddenly be willing to divulge the most sensitive information even to the very detriment of the cause they once stood for but whats more significant than such degenerate behavior is the behavior of the stalwarts, the many who'd rather die and who often do die stubbornly, willingly and lovingly, remaining true to form which selflessly deems betrayals as... "not an option!". This is explained by the Aristotelian Principal perfectly because its nothing less than the individuals own worth and self respect being put on display. A person who maintains his or her own sense of self value and is secure in his or her concepts of what is just and honorable then that person's beliefs will be far too resolute and grounded to be uprooted. Furthermore, that particular plan of life which each individual and the collective rationally chose and agreed upon will be deemed as paramountly worthy and worth carrying out even in the face of sure pain or imprisonment, torture or death. The advent/articulation of this Aristotelian Principal did not bring this behavior into existence but it did fairly analyze it. Such dignity, self respect and inner-conviction has always been around but was never more significant than in the Apostolic times following the death, burial and resurrection of Christ (6 B.C.E. 30 A.D.) because the law and order of these times called for death sentences to all those choosing to remain stalwart believers that Jesus Christ had risen. Not only were most of the Apostles hunted down, imprisoned, beheaded, fed to lions and so forth but these penalties were also visited upon the faithful women, children and scribes as well. Much later this stubborn faith earned its own legal terminology: "The Unimpeachable Witnesses". Their stalwart faith had satisfied the litmus test for discerning Truth from dishonesty by being so unwavering in the face of certain death whereas a dishonest account would usually be flushed out even with just with significant slashes of pain and/ or the mere "threats" of death. e.g. Any rational person today could be taken to a graveyard or morgue then, after witnessing some person raise another person from a confirmably dead state would then have the courage to testify to what he or she just saw, even to a hostile King. Perhaps this rational person knowing his or her testimony will be under the scrutiny of sure death would thoroughly scour and probe the miracle from top to bottom first (the way Thomas did, asking to thrust his own finger into the holes in Jesus' hands and side) but then afterwards, even the most rational person would now have the courage and conviction to write or speak about what he or she saw despite the consequences. So then, in this violently aggressive season of religious intolerance where executions were all creatively diabolical and enthusiastically public, these unimpeachable witnesses pressed forward, spreading the gospel. For the next 30 years immediately after the Crucifixion of Jesus Christ, the apostles were hunted down (in true thug fashion) adapting and embracing this lifestyle of being loved by few, hated by many and respected by all as they kept receiving shelter and warm meals in the underworld communities of every city they went to, constantly dying but (just like the Crips) constantly multiplying like it ain't no thang!

The Aristotelian Principal is just one of many examinations of human ethics and virtues under fire but it has always been important for a man or woman (our type of woman) to have a bedrock set of ethics and virtues because we remain under fire. We are the Apostles of these modern times and we must internalize this Holy Book of Crip Epistles so that our legacy shall one day be reviewed, honored and celebrated as Royal legacies always are. See: Hebrews 11:30-40 (prophecy of our own legacies to come).

The pavements of our concrete jungles all could tell the countless tales of our stubborn faith in the Royal Blue Codes of Courage, Conduct and Criptivity as blood, sweat and bullet shells have been soaked up for decades. Crip scenes have played out exactly the way the scenes of the final days of the apostle's did. In prisons and on death row; in one circumstance a beautiful teenage girl danced to obtain the head of John the Baptist (Salomé, niece of Herod Antipas) only to present it to her mother. James was executed in this same fashion and the one renowned as Apostle number one Peter aprx. 64 A.D. Other lesser known believers suffered equally hideous fates (Bartholemeu-skinned alive, St. Elmo's bowels pulled out on the wheel, etc...). The infamous Roman Saul took part in stoning to death Stephen as he prayed asking for their forgiveness and this feared Saul became the Apostle Paul and got stoned himself, put in prisons, chased out of cities etc... but he kept on traveling. He founded the 1st Christian church at Antioch then he, Barnabas and Mark went out doing missionary work from 46-48 A.D. then returned, scooped up young Silas and took him on missions to Troas, Anthens and Corinth like...."Can't stop! Won't stop!" (49-52 A.D.) They'd all been on Rome's version of America's most wanted so every nation yielded to Rome's authority yet by Paul's third journey (53-57 A.D.) and fourth (59-62 A.D.) four virgin girls stressing, just the way our young Criplettes do so frequently, they begged Paul not to go anymore but Paul responded just the way we all do today and would have back then: "What do yall mean by weeping and breaking my heart? For I am ready not only to be bound but also to die at Jerusalem for the name of the Lord Jesus" (Acts 21:13) and once Paul marched into Rome, he certainly did get bound in prison and wrote several epistles before being put to death between 62-68 A.D. All of these and so many more stalwart believers refused to snitch, break or compromise, demonstrating that self respect which the Aristotelian Principal smiles on, and so their deaths were of worthy consequence for an eternally living, breathing and glowing legacy!!!

300 yrs. later, (after the death of the Roman emperor Aurelian who had been worshiping Mithras the Aryan god of the sun and still up holding the executions of Christians), finally the new Emperor Constantine (306-337 A.D.) issued the edict of Nilan 313 A.D. declaring leniency for Christians (as his Mother was a devout Catholic), Pope Liberius co-opted the December 25th birthday celebration for their old national sun god Mithras to officially represent the birth of Jesus Christ (354 A.D.) Next emperor Theodosius (378-389 A.D.) made Christianity Rome's official religion then finally Pope Damasus 382 A.D. commissioned the blue-blooded Roman Monk St. Jerome to translate the traditional Hebrew text bible into the Latin Volgate bible suitable for Romans to now read. Emperor Constantine had a church built at Peter's burial site (Vatican Hill) which became St. Peter's Basilica lasting aprx. 1200 yrs. All the apostles were sainted as were a few women and other martyrs. The Petrine Text: (Matthew 16:16-19) becomes the holy authority confirming Peter was 1st of the apostles causing even more obsession with the coveted "Apostolic Succession" where being a decendant of any one of the Apostles became like royalty. The blood, sweat and tears of common folks, them

poor and working class disciples was being vindicated, Sainted and now even revered. Common women and men born of harlots and homegirls were able to trace their lineage to Apostle's old safe houses and prison conjugal visits with women of faith who stubbornly kept and bore their children out of wedlock even unaware that those men who were deemed as "outlaws" (of those times) would be recognized as heroes for the infinite amount of tomorrows. However the religious fervor of these monastic times began to burn so hot that every word, every scriptural location, every interpretation and every pronunciation often led to fierce debates, national quarrels, regional slaughters and world wars. Everything from: "Anno Orbis Conditi" (Latin) = Year of Creation of the World. to..."Anno Domini"-Year of our Lord (or of modern era).

Under Greek influences in the early decades before Christ the world was introduced to philosophy, law and government argumentation each of which examines a person or a matter-via-rigorous questions. The Roman era had absorbed these methods and magnified them to an "extreme" that often offends all other religions as even Judaism, after finding sacred epistles (The Dead Sea Scrolls) written by Jesus were probed and accused of plutocracy. Wars and invasions, plagues and pillaging expand from the North and East, the Vikings raping and burning their way to success, Attila leading the Huns into Gual 451 A.D., vandals destroy the Roman fleet 460 A.D. and the dark ages begin and lasts for aprx. 500 yrs. yielding some of the sickest most horrific nonsensical slaughters known to man. Simultaneously an articulate teacher who is believed to have been taught by Angel Gabriel emerges from the Persian region spreading something called Islam, his name... Mohammed (570-632 A.D.). It is believed that he was the final prophet and that to surrender to Allah one must adhere to The Holy Koran and the five pillars of faith beginning with professing there is no God but Allah & Mohammed is his prophet, one must pray five times daily, then "Zakat" = give a portion of your wealth to the needy, one must fast between dawn and dusk during Ramadan and finally (at least once) one must make the Hajj - the pilgrimage to Mecca. Islam successfully carved its way onto the world stage in these dark ages, their Umayyad dynasty (founded 651 A.D. in Damascus) eventually conquers Carthage 694 A.D. and Spain 711 A.D. (saturating Spain with black blooded offspring for 39 yrs.). Various strains of Muslims and various strains of Christians would war relentlessly. Emperors, Kings, Vikings and Anglo-Saxon overlords versus Caliphs, Fatamids (named after Mohammed's daughter Fatima), Turks, and Mongols all vying for land, property and power. Hundreds of years of brutal wars too infinite to cover in this context (even as they continue to this very day) were waged in the name of each group's Religious and/or ethical relativisms. Religious relativisms is of course what branch of the "God Tree" each group believes is the one and only true relative way of life. This then allows a nation to justify its horrific deeds which must fall upon another "unholy" and "cursed" nation or group; it is done under God's Will and by His strength, not theirs.

Ethical Relativism defines what each of these groups and nations deem as moral and right or immoral and wrong which of course they each are only capable of seeing and understanding as it relates to them and their particular ways of life. These conceptualized ways of thinking get craftily articulated into community laws and war prerequisites so that it acts/reacts like a hairpin trigger which fires off at the ready. e.g. a child is held up high in the town square she is screaming and bleeding from a porcupine's vicious assault. Everyone agrees the porcupine did wrong and because it seems to have done this before to others on other occasions it becomes apparent that porcupines are simply immoral and thus the community as good citizens have the moral obligation to form hunting parties to go out in the surrounding woods and rid their land of these vile, evil creatures. This is ethical where its relative to them while in the next town over, the porcupines are celebrated and roam throughout the villages unharmed and unthreatened so they've never had to defend themselves as it is this community's believe that all living things are of God and therefore are good so that it became their law and moral obligation to respect and protect every living thing. War easily ensues when one group of hunters is seen slaughtering their way through the forest that separates their village community from the others village communities. The peace talks often fail because fundamentally their ethical views are too far apart to negotiate terms, boundaries, seasons for killing, etc... This is the ethical relativism which the Crips face. The Consensus have seen a victim of our violence, deemed us as immoral child murderers and set out to destroy us while our ethical view provides that stray bullets have indeed struck unintended targets and children are dying, but it is at the hands of other children merely trying to protect and/or defend themselves. Crips have no such agenda to go out and murder innocent kids no more than the porcupine sets out to find and gore a child. However... living in cold underworld hoods under these cruel circumstances of being Capitalized upon, we stubbornly intend to Believe in ourselves and whats more... we intend to survive by any means necessary! This is what is Religiously and Ethically Relative to the Crips way of life.

"Our Poetic Creed"

Wanting like nature, nothing less than life, wanting Our Love, Life and Loyalty,
> Wanting our existence not to cause strife, wanting the best for this Crips Royalty

Seeing its not in you folks to love, seeing its so in you folks to hate,
> Seeing as you are the chosen from above, seeing how your moral callousness perculate

Hearing how you've ruled the land, hearing how you really get down,
> hearing your: "prisons over education" plan, sharing your hate even without one sound

Feeling your media talking heads, feeling your old hyperbole concern
> Feeling all the life-blood we done bled, feeling the flames from our lives you've burned

Thinking we knew this was what it was, thinking we've done it all before,
> thinking they'd stop when we yell out "cuz!", Thinking so big till' we can think no more...

Tasting the delicious love from our own, tasting the freedom and thrill of the night
> tasting the sweat from our climb to the Throne, tasting the sweetest momentum of Right

Finding it too hard and immoral to snitch, finding it too hard and unethical to cry.
> Finding it so gangster/True Swag to Crip, finding it so True Blue to Live till' we die!!!

Knowing our lifestyles take alot of hard work, knowing its 24/7 without no pay.

Knowing this Crip sex is our sacred perk, knowing Criplettes of all races in it to stay...
Choosing this stand we had to take, choosing this C-Nation to ride hand in hand,
Choosing Death before "Dishonor, make no mistake, choosing to stick to this Crips Script

"The Holy Demand!!!"

II.

Honor. There has always been a sacred code of honor fertilizing the soil upon which we emerged from. Mother earth sopped up the blood, the dripping sweat and the salty tears of ten million slaves who specifically cursed each time a new baby was born, those particular slaves who threateningly raised their clenched fists at the sun in the sky, those who begged God in heaven to one day deliver their children or their children's children from such cold cruelty. Finally honor sprouted up and we came bursting through with our tattooed tears yelling "Death before Dishonor!" Honor is a sense of self respect and dignity which we demand from all others and command from our ourselves collectively and individually. It implies a confidence in one's own ability and self worth, even reinforcing the stability of our personal legacies. Honor is an ancient pillar, the African-Egyptians first made it, then the Greeks, Romans, Persians and Asians all layed it! The Italians, the Portuguese, the Spaniard and the Natives all played it, then throughout the Americas and all of Europe they craftily betrayed it, which is why now the Underworld in both hemispheres secretly display it... The Code of Honor! Long after the Greatest War tactician the old world has ever known, (General Hannibal of Carthage, Spain.) taught the World about Honor (216 B.C.), Long after the Great and fierce Man respectably known as: The Moore of Venice Señor Othello infused Italy with codes of honor it suddenly was needed again in Italy after World War II began. The Mafiusu was a word that roughly meant "Bold" or "Swaggering" during the Italy-Sicily Unification period under Giuseppe Garibaldi but much later while Italians were entangled in World War II abroad their home land was threatened with invasions sparking the call for dedicated Italians to return home to protect "La Cosa Nostra" - (Our Thing) and so it began. Notably one elected official; Prime Minister Giulio

Andreotti clocked billions during his seven terms in office (1972-1992) protected safely by their honor code called the "Omerta" the ultimate oath of silence. Pizzo was paid as everyone understood that Pizzo wasn't just money for protection but moreover was them buying into themselves, their own thing - La Cosa Nostra, despite what they could or could not see, it was that blind faith again (i.e. loyalty). Even after the Capo di tutti (capi = Boss of all Bosses) Salvatore "The Beast" Riina from Corleone was captured in a Palermo Villa, even after the Omerta was clearly broken the spirit of the underworld's code of Honor was just too strong and so it lived on. Honor! The Eastern Hemisphere where ancient codes managed to get passed down from the old Japanese Samurai who would honorably meet on the battlefield, shout out their name, rank, and lineage before then challenging if anyone wanted to come out for a manly engagement on the battlefield. The Katsu Ko Kichi (a young Samurai) and the elders would carry two swords; one large sword for battle and Justice the second sword for their own Seppuku (or Hairekiri) - Suicide by opening ones own abdomen to disembowel the heart. This final act exhibited: "Death Before Dishonor" or punishment of death for ones Dishonor. The Japanese Underworld held fast to codes of Honor as the infamous Yakuzas "today" chop off their own baby finger in front of a round table of elders to genuinely express an apology for committing or allowing the comission of a significant dishonor. In China, their underworld holds fast to the Code of Honor by heeding their infamous Triads who practice and enforce Honor fiercely. The Triads championing secrecy even as seriously as our own Triumvirates. Certain high levels of self discipline are achieved when one develops the strength to do what must be done even when we don't really want to do it. It is a fundamental truth that Love, Life and Loyalty, that Honor and Virtue are family values of excellence which when practiced become second nature. These excellences absolutely must be practiced, upheld and deeply enforced to the letter. We have evolved. Far too many dear loved ones have lost their lives and or their liberty because of our own cousins genuine mistake or miscalculations. Bloopers and Blunders have become far too costly while explanations and apologies have become far too common and casual. The law of nature dictates that everything living or inanimate must experience change; be it fastly and stronger or gradually slow and weaker all things must adhere to change. Everything from the newborn baby to the heavy iron ship anchor rusting and deteriorating on the ocean floor, everything must become more or become less. We this Consolidated Crip Nation have evolved. Sticking to the scriptures, keeping to the Code & holding on to our family values assures us Success and Prosperity. There is no room for: "at least I tried" type lifestyles because for us...Failure is not an option!!! "We must remember the rock (Unity & Secrecy) from whence we were hewn"

-William Still (Father of Underground Railroad)

(Mein true ist mein ehre, und mein ehre ist über alles
"My loyalty is my honor and my honor is above All!!!")

III. Family Values

Having family values, knowing your family's values, practicing and promoting family values are absolutely what deems a people superior to others. Family values are not some silly little pledge or talking point to be murmured throughout some little thug gang in the streets or prisons. Family values are the moral compass each one carries along his or her journey through the forest of life and that compass keeps us on the correct path when those forks in the road appear, when the twists and turns pop up and even when the dirt trails all fade in the brush or at a river's edge, we shall never get lost or led astray.

Our sense of Pride and dignity comes from our overall Honor and Integrity so then, when one has this cloud of pride but has no family values then that pride is as fake as a $6.00 (six dollar) bill. Our honor and integrity is what facilitates our sense of pride even arrogance, our knowing that we're on the right path, we're surrounded by cousins who are on the right path and that eventually we shall all keep achieving our goals of tasting sweet success, knowing all of this tends to make a people proud and make folks a bit boastful. However there are alot of twisted and backwards ideologies being promoted in the hoods. Alot of neologic mindsets that exist today have twisted the old school Crip ways and turned them inwards. Our old school chants that went: "Chitty, Chitty, Bang, Bang, Insane, No Brain, Crip Gang!" are now a justification for fools to simply join us inorder to have a free pass to lose respect for us and kill us. They come on board with the agenda to be celebrated as a crazy ass loco Nut, a cold ass killer who'll shoot anybody, any time, for any reason because real Crips just don't give a fucc. Well, truth is... we were once pushing that way but we had to evolve because alot of good homies and homegirls passed away behind some dumb shit, alot of innocent lives were destroyed over some heat-of-tha'-moment shit and alot of prisons and death rows filled up over some real nonsense that expressed no Honor codes, that protected no lives, that promoted no legacy, produced no dollars and ultimately no sense!

Finally we realize that how we think is not just mildly interesting, how we think is not just a cool subject for intellectual debate but how we think has actually become a matter of life and death. Our biggest task, our greatest objective is to unlearn all the things we've learned under these shrewd former slave owners. It just makes sense for us in a society (system) designed by conquerors where the art of capitalizing upon other's ignorances is thoroughly the way the system works, and being deceived thoroughly is the natural order of the day, and where we find ourselves as the main course dish being so thoroughly fed to that system to keep it alive, it just makes sense for us to step off that system's conveyor belt, and furthermore our duty to unlearn all the poisonous protocols and ideas which that system has implanted in us thoroughly if we intend to someday live.

We'd 1ˢᵗ been spoon-fed the coolness and chivalry of gang life-via-daily T.V. favorites such as: Happy Days, The Duke, Clint Eastwood, Big Valley (westerns) then movies e.g. Grease, Easy Riders, Warriors, American Graffiti, etc... then its glamour was seared into our psyche-via-The Godfather, Scarface, Goodfellas, etc... and finally once it pertained to a certain race, it was vehemently demonized and criminalized-via-T.V.'s popular cop shows: Starsky and Hutch, Adam-12, Baretta, Kojak etc... while in real life the most lucrative prison system on the planet is born-via-The Mass Media and legislation offering zero forgiveness, zero rehabilitations, zero contact family visits and ultimately zero Habeas Corpus Appeals (per. 1997-Anti-Terrorist law way before we knew what a real Terrorist was). These Holy Scriptures can't address all the deceptions subliminally put in place but urge that we review (through positive eyes) the 2001 Columbia movie "Baby Boy". You'll see.

Our urbanized ethics and morals are detectable through dialogue given by O.G's as father figures, by Momma as a Mother in law former youngster, from homeboy to homeboy about the plight of not wanting to be dependent on the girlfriend and her Mother, praying not to end up hurting no one, then its seen in the love-hate dialogue our girls often display as well as the reaction when a fellow Crip breaks the Code. The Community is overwhelmingly populated with real men affording locs to have the benefit of several dads big brothers and uncles but society was duped and dupes itself to believe men abandon their family regularly. Our own community looks to law enforcement to help vanquish the Crips without realizing we are the last and final frontier for urban family values and structure. Society has become emotionally invested in undoing us-via-govt. sanctions and (Life-until-death) prison sentences all while according to Ralph Nader sources (F.B.I. reports) street crime nationwide costs aprx. .4 Billion a year while white collar crime costs $200 Billion per year and gets ignored by the media and the govt. Tobacco kills ten times more (innocent lives). Legal foods and drugs kills another ten times more, alcohol another huge population and according to the Russell Mokhiber corporate crime report almost 60,000 Americans die from job related disease and accidents and the O.S.H.A. (Occupational Safety Health Admin.) buys political and media silence regularly. We have got to elevate our way of thinking. An attack on the Crips is a calculated attack on the only urban family structure most "left behind" children have ever had and ever will have. It is all of our jobs to do better. Here in lies just a few key kernels offering wisdom filled scripture for elder Men as our Nation's fathers, for our Nations elder women as Crip Mothers, for our young locs both male and female and obviously for us All because family Values are for Everyone, because Love, Life and Loyalty aren't exclusive to no one under the Royal Blue banner. If you've read the Script, stick to the script even Excellently!

The Values and Morals of a family absolutely begins and ends with the Man. God created man to be the head of the family. He designed men with "Alpha-Male" characteristics and potential however this ancient knowledge initially was stolen but even now it largely remains hidden from the general population, the middle class and lower class in particular because they are unable to afford the Elite Education that teach certain truths. It profits no one to empower (by educating) lower or middle working class people about their alpha-male-inner qualities and how to properly use those qualities because economically there is so much money to be made off the backs of ego-maniacs and ignorant fools. The Creator never intended for life to be this way but it is. Initially our duty as man was as simple as the four P's: Proclaim, Procreate, Provide and Protect. From apes and lions to bulls and birds, once the male proclaims his love (or intentions) the female yields and her willingness to yield is largely predicated on her perception about "if" he is going to follow through "Excellently" on the "providing" and "protecting" once she's vulnerable with hungry infants (or delicate eggs). Finally the Elite among us is stepping back up, evolving and right now matured enough to "stick to the Script"! The Orders of the day are: Love, Life, and Loyalty!

I Corinthians 13:11 "When I was a child, I spoke as a child, I understood as a child, I thought as a child; but when I became a man, I put away childish things."

Without Love it is impossible to Lead, Without Life it is impossible to Live, Without Loyalty it is impossible to Last! So then, as men, our first duty is to lead and promote love till death. Love is much more than physical lust or emotional adoration. Love is much more than bomb sex or the beautiful articulation of words and although Love may embody any combination of these traits it is all of these and so much more and so to put it best we've very carefully concluded that Love...Real Love, is absolutely a Commitment! and therefore Crip Love is the ultimate commitment, pledge and oath that can never be minimized. It is because this doctrine. Love, Live and Loyalty is just so essential to being a True Blue, we must understand each component, crystalize each component and then be able to absorb completely and Overstand each component within this doctrine. Cowardly Commitments are modified and/or broken regularly by the mere mortals and civilians but with us a commitment must be honored Excellently. We as evolved mature adults (men, women and children) shall up hold and commit to the standard of Excellence in everything we say and do. This Commitment to Excellence allows us more assurance and trust in each other, no doubts because we are certain that any true cousin that sticks to the Script will only say what he or she means and will mean what he or she says, period! We can invest our faith and whole heart in any project that a cousin is proposing because our high standards of Excellence dictate that we know our craft & we master whatever trade skill we're blessed with. We love (with Crip love) our particular role on our particular team within the hood faculty and we play that position of ours excellently. No bloopers or blunders, no "I'm sorry" or "oops, my bad", no honest mistakes and no shortcomings. This is the Multi-Million and Billion dollar lessons one thoroughly learns during those years in Ivy

League universities. Meanwhile, the rest of the world perpetuates doctrines of failure by repeating such slogans like: "We're only human!", "You can only do your best!" "Everybody makes mistakes" and "You can't win 'em all!". These slogan are genocidal poisons. It provides a soft cushion for failures to land on and removes the dire determination and drive required in life to succeed. Our men were being misled by our dearly loved and trusted women who innocently taught us what she'd heard from the deceptive media and brainwashed pastors. Then as impressionable young boys we are spoon fed genocidal poisons about what defines a man, warped slogans that sound good but do bad such as: "Real men stand all alone" or... "When you become a man you don't have to do what your parents say or what nobody say" and "Real men follow their owns rules" etc... These slogans have cemented rudeness, chaos, dissension, ignorance and arrogant misdirection in the hoods making self destruction a lifestyle. Meanwhile the graduates from the most prestigious "Higher learning" centers (i.e. Colleges) emerge and put into practice all the opposites of our slick-sounding ghetto slogans. They don't believe "everyone makes mistakes". "You can't win'em all" and so forth. They learn to walk into a billion dollar corporations and promise the C.E.O. (via-his College resumé) that they represent "Excellence!" period! The doctrine of excellence that insists on winning and chants "failure is not an option!" This is the Royal Blue cloth that Crip Love shall be cut from and what shall keep us all bound together... Love Excellently! Life. Love for Life! Life is the second of our triple "L" doctrine but this second component can not be divorced from the three because they depend on each other and together function as One. Life is much more than just a series of inhales and exhales, Life (as a gift) was given to mankind to signify much more than whatever particular amount of cash each person can gather up then die with. In actuality Life is about "Living" and Living has its own components that of course may include those apparent vanities but oh so much more especially for people like us who are collectively more intimately aware life is fragile. Life for us is the actual forward momentum and dynamic activity of Living and Living is the performances and executions of virtuous duties that both compliment and fulfill us and our Legacy. Life for us is a journey which ultimately ends at the destination of death, there is no other apex or climax we see life moving towards therefore when we are in motion it seems we are moving buck wild and fancy free. However we maintain our core values (and ours alone) in this group dynamic process of Living Life. "Therefore I say to you, do not worry about your life, what you will eat; nor about the body, what you will put on. Life is more than food, and the body is more than clothing" Luke 12:22-23 Finally, the third "L" and final prong to this Love, Life and Loyalty doctrine is of course: LOYALTY. The essential and defining component to Loyalty is the ability to stand firm and hold fast to blind faith. Loyalty is more than a chant of sweet sounding words but requires a display of what we describe as our: "Minds of Steel, Hearts of Stone!". We are not able to be swayed in situations and circumstances where doubt and disbelief are being weaponized. All manner of agents and foreign enemies are trained with tactics to weaponized ones natural human inner-thoughts about people, places, things and ideas that aren't solid concrete and evident but as the Aristotelian Principle already reminded us; an individual's personal conviction and belief in what they're doing or what the over all life-plan being carried out by their collective group, this will ultimately determine a person's threshold for how far their loyalty to their people or that life-plan shall go. Having minds of steel means that we know with blind certainty that our life plan is toward our own Legacy collectively and individually and there are no soft spots to penetrate our Minds of Steel just as the Love shall not penetrate a heart of stone. Love is the Commitment, Life is the dynamic activity of our Commitments to Excellence and Loyalty is the motivating faith and stubborn belief in ourselves collectively and individually which makes us secure in our steps progressing ever forward. Love, Life and Loyalty yields for us the one REAL pay off that human existence shall be measured by the one thing that sets humans apart from all of Gods other creations allowing us to show full appreciation for this gift of Life, that one real pay off is called: LEGACY.

The one shining beacon of proof that God's gift was had shall be our forever lasting Legacy so our Love, our Lives and our Loyalty facilitates eternal life after death just as it was ordained to do. And so it is written: "Without Love, one can't lead, without Life, one can't Live, without Loyalty, one can't Last!!!"

Mothers. Family values as they apply to a Mother also differ from those designed by the civilian world because a Crip Mother is always a Mother by choice and pure deliberateness. We certainly do honor both Mothers and Fathers (Ephesians 6:2) the way the civilian world says they do but because the Crip Mommas share in our Commitment to Excellence and take seriously the doctrine of Love, Life and Loyalty we regard our Mothers in a much higher, more aggressive esteem and honor. They've been our Queen Jewels of the Nile every since Egypt called her name 2100 B.C. (in the 1st dynasty) on the African Continent while Europeans in the North were clubbing their women over the head and dragging her unconscious body back to his cave. The Crip Mother is the very first teachers we get from birth and it carries on from the womb to the tomb.

The general role of any teacher is to change the student, the pupil, the learner in some way which is why the relationship with the Crip Mother is so important and serious. A youthful mind functions like a sponge constantly soaking up information whether it is supposed to or not. Therefore these very first teachers, the Crip Mothers are expected to mold and change us for the better. She must be thorough and clear with the young boys in regards to what is deplorable from what is honorable because mixed messages certainly cost folks their lives later on. The Crip Mothers must above all stress to the male child that being humble and having discipline is not a sign of someone weak but actually its a characteristic of the strong. She must be very careful and refrain from telling every male child to "be a leader...be your own man!" because maybe as many as 3 out of 10 boys are born leaders at the most while the rest must fall in line and play their position confidently. It is simply irresponsible to press our ill-tempered and unqualified sons and baby brothers to have unrealistic aspirations of leadership because their successes and greatest legacy might be found in their service and team spirit which they will never embrace unless Crip Momma teaches him to.

The C-Mother's bigger, much more critical teaching task is the schooling of the female child. Girls who become women are quietly our Crip Essence in the flesh. The female Crip is essentially the fire that can either burn strong within us or burn away our internal ties which bind us together.

Fire when it is contained and controlled can protect and warm a family through our winter storms, it can feed us, kill off the bacteria from our proteins and refine even our souls the way it refines all other precious metals but fire can also destroy any and everything it touches. Fire uncontained or controlled has an insatiable appetite and can't help but devour and destroy everything.

These fires, in true Crip fashion won't ever want to be controlled, they're uncomfortable with any level of their freedoms being tamed and actually they feel most alive when they're burning fast, burning wild and burning free but because of the many flammable moving parts within the Cadre and the C-Nations our sweet and beautiful flames must stick to the script and obey Moms, as the saying goes...The Crip Mothers always know best how to handle her own candles and so it is these in particular that she must. It is also essential for the Crip Mothers to remind the girls that while they are doing right to encourage and support anarchy, it must never be at work within our ranks, our own community, our own family because it is collectively that we are the anarchy out from under the governments who choose to despise us. Many Cadres were the source of their very own destruction simply because their girls were attracted to and rewarded dishonorable acts and were decidedly supportive of transgressors and cowards over our own Holy Scriptures.

Society concedes that no one understands the female wiles or the female ways but the Crips have made no such concession. We understand her fully as the walking, talking, living, breathing chaos agent that she is and we adore her for it, all of it, but only because it moves in sync with our masculine nature to rescue her, to impress her, to feed her and to make everything outside our world bow down to her. She is the fire within us but unschooled by the Crip Mothers she will almost certainly take to burning down her own home, the Cadre itself. (e.g. Most young Criplettes enjoy having the off and on switch to her Crip's rage so at any given time she may decide to sex up or flirt with the one fellow comrade her dude don't get along too well with, then boom! Chaos! Young Criplettes will challenge and question her dude's manhood based on his Loyalty and commitment to his comrade and although she knows the script she claims he needs to stop following everything that cuz say "like a lil bitch!". Her nature is chaos, drama and destruction but we know her well as do the Crip Mothers who once were them and for this reason we entrust the C-Mothers to correct their paths as frequently and as constantly as necessary because it is for her own good. The very first white Criplette, Vanilla Child-Lady-T

(Teena Marie) sang about the fire with Rick and escaped the deep west Los Angeles Shoreline in Venice but everybody knew she was no square. We love all our females for real but she must never allow her flames to turn inward because for the good of the Nation and in compliance with our Love, Life and Loyalty, before any candle can burn down the entire Crip Mansion it most certainly shall be blown out. Crip Mother even said so...

Young Locs. Family values found in the hearts and the minds of the Youngs these days are much different from the family values you'd have found in us back in the mid-80's however that core temperament is still there. That same: "I don't give a fuck!" and "I'll flash on yo' ass quick!" Mentality still plagues the Youngs, the locs and the lettes but we simply on another level with it now. The level we on now is all about dollars, scratch, paper, marbles or whatever other slick name you want to use and the integrity part, the Crip family values are in the back seat while money is doing all the driving. Stanley Tookie William's last request to alot of us whom had successfully evolved; "Y'all who know better, go ahead and Do Better!" which we adopted as our final Orders and duty to the kids, to our youth & the Crip Nasty Youngs! Excellence!

Reclaiming our core family values of Honor and Crip integrity shall not abandon or deny the values that dominate today but our values are gonna take back over the steering wheel and allow the almighty dollar to hit the backseat or roll shotgun but for sure money is staying in the Crip Car. We've put everything back into its proper perspective because all these new-booty hood rules got it all twisted out of order for example: "Money and Power!" is a blooper because money can't never land before power and these days it always do which is why those with money gotta flee for they life or work with the police because money without the proper power to demand that it be respected is really nothing more than a cool jack move waiting to happen. Its no wonder ballers are in bullet-proof vehicles speeding through the turfs he or she once called home, they got the money before securing the power. Its no wonder we see movie after movie of the cut throats getting their own throats cut by their childhood friends or snitched on and testified against by their own family, their own neighbors... Money before the Power.

Another family value which has been chronologically twisted is the M.O.B. idea. Money over bitches is what it preaches. It certainly sounds slick enough so its gotta be true, plus it makes a lil sense for a true to chase his paper first before he chase a bitch. Any pimp or player will tell you that when you're chasing the bitch, you're running away from the money but if you just chase yo' money then or damn sure the bitches will be chasing you! So its M.O.B. right? Wrong because the Crips gotta' see this shit through real eyes and realize the Real lies!!! Truth is, most Crips are gonna have a bitch way before we can even imagine what real money looks like and for us, them bitches who soldier through them broke and hungry times is gonna have her a seat at the table once its time to ball and thats no matter what because its all a part of Love, Life and Loyalty! We bring honor back into the game so let the new booty fools pop-off about MO.B. and we'll baptize they bitches with this Crippin' and end up with his money and his bitch on some real live: "The World is Ours!" type shit. Its no wonder females is twisting fools out there and forming their own crews. Rogue ghetto bitches holla'ing "flame on!"

Another backwards philosophy out there that sounds slick enough and seems like its pretty true is: CREAM Cash Rules Everything Around Me! Anybody with common sense will just look at the world around him or her and agree that cream is just keepin' it real, it appears to just be true so if cash rules everything around us then getting our money has got to make 1st sense, common sense certainly but ain't nothing common about the Crips or the senses we'll have to tap into in order to excel. Our commitment to excellence requires us to employ much higher senses than those that are common because success is shaped like a Triangle and the base of it begins with the most general, indeed the most common and then thins out dramatically the higher you climb towards prosperity. In other words these common notions about having to first get the money is the common recipe for disaster and failure. When we, the Crips look with our Real eyes, we can realize the Real lies and see that those in the real world, with real money are able to enjoy it for real because it is established after real power. e.g. you place twin females, dressed in the same clothes in different environments, one in the hoods, one in the halls of congress, both are wearing an identical million dollar diamond necklace and carrying an expensive purse with a million dollars cash inside. In one setting she and the money is safe because of the power and in the other not only is she immediately rushed and robbed of all her valuables but even the robbers are later found dead and death follows the necklace and the cash each time it surfaces or echoes prices to be sold or the cash is being spent. Over the course of a considerably short time, both the necklace and the money in the hood settles evenly or is grinded down into small enough portions where it causes no more lives to be taken, no more twists and betrayals because a million people each end up with one dollar, hardly enough to effect change or cause any more violence over. Meanwhile, where there is power first, the money is allowed to exist in its bulk form and death nor betrayals have to come into play because everyone recognizes that there is a collective purpose at work, there is a collective power they all must protect to keep honor alive. This is not merely a test that fails because the hoods are poor and hungry because those same identical girls, dressed the same, both wearing the million dollar necklace, both carrying the same purses full of cash could travel safely to other poor places and not be rushed and robbed cuz even poor people must have a code of honor to respect and live by. Every hood, community and domain MUST have codes of honor established otherwise it don't belong to them nor they to it. The True Sicilians can state flatly "Nobody harm this girl or touch her necklace or purse full of money" and in the poorest part of Sicily shes safe, the same for Yakuzas in ghetto Japan areas, the Zulu's in their tribal South African areas, the Triads in the poor areas of China, the elite bosses overseeing the poorest Farvellas in Brazil or certain rude-boy Rastafarians overseeing them glorious Blue Mountains of Jamaica even the Secret Service and the Secret Society overseers for the White House and England. Power generates honor and integrity which in turn establishes overall safety and security for everyone.

Very few Crip Communities still enjoy these luxuries but as we return to the Script, we all shall again. Our ranks were damaged by the crack and crack-baby-era where everybody has ADD or ADHD but attention deficit hyperactive disorders can be cured. The young homies and homegirls who know within their own hearts that they have a tendency to flash or fly off the handle are herein being called on to self check and/or get themselves treated not out of fear but out of Love, Life and Loyalty to Crip. There is nothing fancy or honorable or even unique about you reaching that point where you're like: "I don't give a fuck!" however, from the date the holy Crip scriptures hit yo' hood, you should know that excellence is now expected of you and so, not giving a fuck is saying fuck all that is True Blue. Our values have suffered long enough and now its time to restore honor and integrity where it belongs. Games and Bloopers and the overall lack of seriousness have all run their courses so that now, even if you are a parent, child or sibling-via-D.N.A. you are now officially on notice to step yo' game up or step yo' ass out because living is expensive, mistakes are too costly and death is entirely too cheap and basically free! How you gonna marvel at Mafia Movies about Irish, Italians or Russians but then twist a black in Royal Blue and call it just for fun-zees like all these over crowded cemetery parks and morgues ain't a testament to the truth. Fathers stop raising your kids under such illusions, Mothers stop filling your sons and daughters with so much disregard and hate for the code merely because you had a tough time. Even our own upper and middle class wealthy blacks with education have to get their rhetoric of defamation pointed elsewhere, self-hate should be beneath you by now. We evolved as you asked us to, as our black president and 1st Lady asked us to, as the 1st black Attorney General Eric Holder asked us to and most of all as the laws of nature created by God demanded we do, grow stronger or begin to deteriorate growing weaker. From the Arab Spring to the Occupy wallstreet's fall we've grown and so no longer can we play dumb or crazy and no longer can we pretend that deliberate indifference towards us as human beings is acceptable. From the Young locs to the senior O.G's we shall finally prioritize our "Go getting" more thoughtfully as it is written: "Happy is the Crip who finds wisdom and the hood star who gains understanding; for her proceeds are better than the profit of silver, and her gains than fine gold" (Proverbs 3:13-14).

Family values shall be thoroughly practiced, established and protected before the purse because paper has only poisonous value when there are no established concrete family values in place. For Example: Two families each made up of one million people: 250,000 elder men, 250,000 elder women 250,000 young guys, 250,000 young girls in both family "A" and in family "C". You rain down one million dollar bills on family "A" with no family values then on family "C" with Crip family values. Both are aware that this is free money which no one man has more claim to than the next. So, family "A" explodes into utter chaos and violence; every man, woman and child for himself shouting "Get Yours!" because "money is king" and get it "by any means necessary!". Meanwhile, family "C" having Crip family values naturally has a faculty who everyone trust in blind faith as they assemble a faculty meeting then by consensus they decide to only break the entire million into four equal parts, one portion going into stocks & bonds, another portion is directed into the family treasury which is like the pulse of the entire "C" family, the third portion goes to the Investments and fundraisers team who immediately facilitates carnivals and concerts with all the top entertainers of the day (scheduled in our honor) generating major funds to replenish the family businesses and connections, the final portion goes directly towards the immediate needs of all nine of the family's faculty teams. This would be called: "functionalism" in Ivy League college language while what occurs in family "A" would be called: Disfunctional or "disasterous" in any language. The very best case scenario for family "A" with no values is that everyone could walk away with their single dollar bill while the more probable outcome is that multiple small bands of the strong members of family "A" will set out to jack and take it all to be split amongst their crew, however... chaos breeds chaos and violence begets violence. Ultimately the strong take to killing off one another, the weak and innocent who aren't cowering away in the shadows of their own neighborhoods eventually take sides or become collateral damage in a permanent war-zone where death and betrayals follow the multiple portions of money that still remains. Family "A" is just a fictional example for the purposes of these Scriptures but these Crip families and ghetto group dynamics are certainly real and for those who doubt. Just scout for Exhibit "A" which may be that ghetto hood near you. Its no wonder the ballers usually flee the hood, the successful athletes and entertainers you grew up with have to run for their lives as soon as the check is cut, its no wonder the hood property values decrease regularly, the mom and pop businesses dry up regularly, the college graduates and educators abandon ship to rather teach and educate those other people's children, securing every other people's future but their own, our political minds draft legislation that attacks their former neighborhoods, our children that were sent away cowering find their perfect fit in the local police departments where revenge becomes the sweetest taste they ever had. The media enjoys exploiting the urban "disfunctional" family and as a result of their indifferences toward us, our actors and actresses can't excel by having such a rich plethora of stories to tell and sell. The absence of family values becomes detrimental to us all so then, as our ways of thinking have evolved so must our overall agendas. Our success shall not send us running for the hills to live in gated communities that can only just barely stomach the sight of us. Proudly we're finally equipped to rebuild our own communities, restore our own businesses and allow the faculty to re invest in our own architects and construction companies to finally enjoy the sweet tasting success of functionalism in the hoods who stick to the Script and keep family values. Love, Life and Loyalty! The Commitment to Excellence! And Death before Dishonor! Holding fast to our family values not only guarantees a progressive cycle of finances will drive up the economy, the jobs and the real estate (functionalism) but it also shall end the social onslaught of our dead and defenseless icons. Michael Jackson was the only Super star who specifically selected us, visited our concerts at Mardi Gras and the Coliseum where we did the Crip walks and the back slide (moon walk). He displayed us in his videos when the media told everyone that "Deliberate indifference" was the new plan. The defamation of President and First Lady O, these constant slants against Whitney Houston, these harshly framed discourses against our athletes, singers, actors, producers for any small mistakes, the countless displays of psychopathic dispositions would all end once we, the backbone of a rich passionate people, yea...The Crips return with our true family values dipped in Royal Blue.

Prescribed Movies: Drumline
                      Blue Hill Ave

IV. Deliberate Indifference (I.E. Disregard)

We've been forced to finally address disregard as it is being so thoroughly and so deeply systematized into each and every thread that forms the fabric of America. It is at this point in history that we see the tragic results of disregard as it is being routinely practiced by a society unknowingly plagued by and/or with psychopathic behaviors.

First there is the Political Spectrum where society is lead to believe that we're witnessing the complete range of interests from one extreme to the other. Polar opposites called the left and the right, the Blue and the Red, the liberals and the conservatives and this is the perfect balance we are being represented within. However, if one were to listen to the politicians closely, (even our own Prez. Obama), you'd hear the right wing seeming partial to the wealthy or upper class while the left wing the middle class or the blue-collar working class and at best they'll come together with resolve somewhere in the upper middle. Meanwhile... the massive majority (often referred to as the minorities) have no candidate and are disregarded by design of the Real Politik. 1498 Niccoló Machiavelli came up with their modern form of political thinking called "Realism" which is to say: "The ends justifies the means." The ends is: conquest, The means is: Force, The ends is basically a decision of what kind of society you want or what ultimate goal or outcome you desire. The means is simply to decide what you do to achieve or get it! "...it seems more proper to me to go to the truth of the matter than to its imagination....for we live so far removed from how we ought to live, that he who abandons what is done for what ought to be done, will rather learn to bring about his own ruin than his preservation" - Niccolo Machiavelli. But the problem with the seductive sounds of this

Realism, especially for us as Crips is that once we accept the reasonable notion that you shall base your decisions on "Reality = (this is just the way that it is)" you're accepting without question someone else's version of what reality is, of what your reality is and must remain in comfortable service positions to their best interests, their reality! In truth, the world is complex and realities differ, so, to believe that we all have the same interests in our slums, ghetto communities and third world islands as they do who report the news, who make the laws, the prisons and the corporations that thrive successfully, to believe we have the same values is delusional and tragically "un"realistic. The media. The networks, the politicians, the food industry, drug industry and all the multi-billion dollar corporations pay millions to be represented by special interest groups and political activist committees whom had better produce results they can profit from and there is no such results where all of them can profit and continue to thrive and also make the poor and lower-middle class succeed as well. In reality we are disregarded and absolutely deceived by design, the doctrine Machiavelli called: The Lion and The Fox, He explains that the government should emulate both! The Lion uses force; (impose your will!) because...fortune is a woman and it is necessary, if you wish to master her, to conquer her by force...The fox is more cunning and instead uses deception Machiavelli rationalizes it carefully as he explains: "If all men were good this would not be good advice but since they're dishonest and do not keep the faith with you, you in return need not keep faith with them and no Prince was ever at a loss for plausible reasons to cloak a breach of faith... The experiences of our time shows those Prince's to have done the great things (historically) those who had little regard for good faith and who had been able by astuteness to confuse men's brains". This and many other doctrines of Realisms set every man, woman and child on a course of conquest that fueled slavery, expansionism and world dominance at the expense of the people of color yet the one color that won't be tamed is of course the boys and girls in royal blue. It is with Real Eyes that we've realized the Real lies which had us deceived and cooperatively disregarded, and so now their politics and the real politik all mean one thing to us Real Poli-tricks and tricks are for kids! It is at this point of awareness that we chant proudly "Minds of steel, hearts of stone" knowing now that Blue Steel is more than just a gun, it is the assault rifle that is our minds!!! So...as the Nation sees through all the media and political propaganda put out there to deceive and disregard, we know that our seeing it constitutes: CHECK #1.

Second after the political spectrum we must see the whole Economical spectrum world wide. It should and shall be abundantly clear to all cousins within the Consolidated C-Nation that our Misfortune is the cornerstone of any economy structured to capitalize off its own citizens. We kill and die to purchase their expensive, overpriced shoes, clothes, jewelry, cars and homes meanwhile they still disregard us. When we wanted decent jobs they rejected us for having one ear pierced, tattoos, oversized pants and a proud attitude, now almost thirty years later the neo-hip hop era with kids on college campuses and in the suburbs adorning everything that we were disregarded and rejected for, they're suddenly being recognized as just good, decent kids who deserve a break and these "new" styles are something they all invented. Economically we must remain vilified inorder to provide "well meaning" to all their sweeping "tough decisions" that disregard the poor and abandon the struggling lower class folks all alike. It was for us, the early-mid 80's when certain hoods were given huge trash-bin dumpsters full of guns. As a teenager we thought of how lucky we were, we were the only hood I knew of who had came up on some police station or any base's lil blooper disposal mission for these guns and when we told the big homies what we'd found we were largely pushed out the way and never saw the guns again and were cool with the pistols we had smartly and routinely skimmed off the top for ourselves so it never became a big deal as guns were mainly for show. We'd pull it to expedite a robbery quickly without no physical effort, we'd pull it to disperse huge gang brawls at after school spots and we'd show'em to friends we each had on the civilian side to sorta' enhance their fascination at what life must be like as a member of the Crips. None of us had a clue that congress had split hairs with President Reagan about the federal money going into Nicaraguan harbors for alleged mining projects, we'd never heard about no general[21] Westmoreland or any of the governments guns programs in exchange for hostages or being dealt to the Nicaraguan Contras after a re-elected Reagan and newly-elected Gorbachev had their

---

[2] [1] General William Westmoreland later in 1986 theorized it as a post WWII obligation stating: "U.S.A. inherited the mantle of leadership of the free world" and "became the international champions of liberty."

"summit". Economically none of us knew warehouses of cocaine were being made available in other Crip hoods simultaneously & that fashion would suddenly become either Royal Blue or blood red (Pumas shoes, Fila wear, snakeskin belts, fat-lace shoestrings, leather bomber jackets etc...) as the movie called "Colors" tried to tell one of our stories (even to the real rap lyrics of a genuine native named Ice-T) and none of us knew that several years later[32] Oliver North Jr and President Reagan would have to spend alot of their political currency and admit there were secret operations during their handling of the Iran-Contra Costa war that got out of control. Economically we never knew that all these imported foreign guns and drugs destroying our community (generation by generation) were funding black operations for the government, the very same government that accused us of being menaces to society & homegrown terrorist, we just never knew economically that there was an unseen hand and we never calculated the total gross that must've been accrued as we saturated 41 states with our Crip blue magic and megalomania-swag in hundreds of cities and towns in those states, we just never calculated the reality that, in order for so many of us Crips to be ballin' out of control, from hundreds of different sets even, that somebody had to be at the tip top of the pile, that somebody had to be harvesting fields and fields, that somebody had to be in laboratories turning the shit into powder before we got it and economically somebody was really and truly ballin' but on a whole-nother-level until ultimately our own cousin Rich ass freeway Rick Ross shed some blue light on the situation, now we know! Real eyes, Realize, Real lies!!! Fortunately being economically exploited and disregarded has obviously taught us a thing or two and so now there will be no next time, because from this time forward we're sticking to the script and we're each very well equipped with our own tools (the Faculty) and knowledge to legally accrue our own wealth and support our own businesses and networks which will allow us to pay homage and high regards to ourselves. The media shall never humanize us just as surely as they will never demonize their own. The system is by design.

"The functioning role of the Media is to inculcate and defend the

---

[32] Colonel Oliver North - National Security Council staff member was charged in the covert operations of delivering military supplies to the counter revolutionary groups in Nicaragua after Congress made such aid illegal.

economic, social and political agenda of privileged groups that dominate the domestic society and the state".

- (Noam Chomsky & Edward Herman)

Chomsky and Herman provided multiple (documented) examples of how differently the media treated historical events (careful wordings and framings) such as Racism, the Tet offensive during the Vietnam war, the Watergate scandal (Nixon era) and the Iran Contra (Reagan era). If folks just received a better history education, if folks just learned to look beneath the surface of all these assigned labels, if folks just understood that our Nation's American and European Orthodoxy (<u>orthos</u> = right, <u>doxa</u> = opinion) is required and prefers to conceal certain facts about our Society, if folks just knew that much about history they might then react with anger towards all the homelessness, the poverty and the despair that plagues millions of folks instead of crushing the budgetary back of education programs to fund prison development instead of blaming the Crips for society's decline, folks might question how did those inner-city youth get German lugars, Middle Eastern assault rifles and how did we discover how to make coca-fields into powders and rock cocaine or poppy-fields into heroin? These are questions no media would ever ask but it will gladly and routinely broadcast crime rates and the need for longer prison terms and zero parole for us old men serving life. With just a bit of effort folks could find out the numbers the media is keeping concealed such as the State of California alone has spent over 9.6 billion dollars on prisons but barely 5.7 billion on the entire U.C. system and state colleges. Or the fact that as of 2012 California has built only one college since 1980 but in the same time frame has built 21 prisons even economically disregarding the fact that a college student cost the state 8,667 while each prisoner costs the state 45,006, wow indeed! The cold Truth is, journalist as well as historians must select what they think is important or what they think the public will consider important or what the publishers will deem important before they work on it. Often they will just report on something because everyone else before them had written and/or reported on it and they will omit something because it has always been omitted. There is certainly a conservative bias in place to filter any and everything written or broadcast that might disrupt the systems social construct. Let's be clear, the founding fathers who drafted and signed into existence the U.S. Constitution were wealthy elder white men whose objective was not to put in place a system which would then suddenly reduce them and their wealth down to levels any and everyone could easily rival or obtain lest we forget that these were men just emerging from Europe, the old world where medieval tortures, with hunts, conquest and tyranny were the norm. There was no history of kindness and compassion, generosity or goodness from which they could draw inspiration from, there was no overwhelming religious conviction that drove them more than it was their own rich leadership skills and decisive empirical visions that captured opportunity in the face of adversity. From the very first: "We the People" of the Preamble all the way to the Pledge of Allegiance to the flag vowing "liberty and justice for all", no faces of color was pictured to be included although each of them had several hundred hands and eyes cooking, cleaning, working and being Nanny to their seed, economically we were disregarded and that Constitutionalized system still disregards us even to this day. For example: (1) The Marketing professionals and U.S. Corporation's professor's in advertisement regularly send out books of coupons to over 725,000 "selected" families which they call "connectors" but no handouts for folks "like us". (2) The Federal Communications Commissions and Nielson ratings systems regularly survey over 500,000 "selected" families each season to serve their system of tailoring T.V. broadcastings according to the same old empirical social order that disregards folks "like us"! (3) U.S. Department of Agriculture provides millions and millions in aid and incentives as well as huge tax cuts, protections and non-intrusive perks for "selected" families who shall stay in place as the "rural class" doing prosperity work, casually disregarding "folks like us". (4) The Federal Deposit Insurance Corporation (F.D.I.C.) inventories and investigates annually over one million accounts for fines and prosecutions, finally the "selected" families are the "folks like us". (5) U.S. Department of Justice designs and deploys multiple agenda notices supporting all of their agencies, task forces, peace officers, parole boards, guards, unions and victim advocacy groups that all function under incentives and meeting quotas that target "selected" folks "like us". So there are these and too many other systematic norms in place to count, but it is evident that they founding fathers constitutionalized a system which would protect their selected "We the People" without disturbing their god-given-right (even their duty) to capitalize off of the disregarded "folks like us" whose ignorance makes it all work. The system functions sorta' like a basic seesaw where one side (the heavier, greater, more populace side) must stay positioned at the poor-dirty ground level allowing the opposite side (the lighter, more affluent, selected few) to stay positioned up high soaring in the blue skies. To be honest, it's fair to say that this system wasn't predicated on racism because at the time there were plenty of whites in position to be anchored at the bottom as paupers. Finally Abraham Lincoln was forced to speak to the situation in a presidential debate against Douglas in Springfield Ill. (1857-58) after the Supreme Court had already ruled that a slave is not a real U.S. citizen. Lincoln walked the line with a dissociation styled speech where he NEVER said Blacks were their equals but spoke "economically" INRE: the system in place and reasoned that "the government cannot endure permanently half slave and half free." and he merely proposed that Blacks be allowed the chance (economically) to pursue upward mobility i.e. get yourselves a f**cing job! This is such a genius approach because it suggests that nepotism wasn't being practiced all of a sudden and that the burden of survival would from here on be on the backs of the inferior minded folks who dared to ask for such responsibility. It was this type of genius rhetoric that is still celebrated today because it remains the most elegant dissociate prose to be delivered and it allows everyone to hear exactly what they want to hear and be satisfied. Everyone believes Prez. Lincoln was on their side, speaking in their best interests but the end result should be evidence enough of where he stood. The System as it functions "today" is admittedly in favor of upward mobility but, it should and shall be pursued-via-Education. It shall devour the uneducated without mercy. The system is to provide this required higher and highest learning at an inflated cost so that in essence its not actually within everyone's reach. So... for the "select few" who can afford the highest, their children shall ultimately have the same good fortune and so on, then for the "select few" who has the best grades and is favored by chance they will be selected to recieve financial aids and student loans which will require the better portion of their entire lives to fully pay off yet they will have realized the dream just enough to be able to look back at all those they'd left behind in the slums and say: "see...its possible! the system really works!" But in real math anyone can see that not everyone can go to college even if every high school somehow turned out 85% (for just one semester) all the colleges are already full and jobs already far in between, so this system was never designed to withstand such a huge impact, even for one semester. Theodore Roosevelt (Prez. 1901-09) endorsed a racist book called: "The passing of the great race" By. Madison Grant who suggested that immigrants be put to death inferring the wave of nepotism had even spurred the government to set limits of 4,000 per year from Italy, 2,000 from Russia; China and Palestine were limited to 100 immigrants per year while of course (two of the system's favorite racist gene pools sources) Great Britain was allowed 34,000 per year and Germany a whopping 51,000 per year, both of which are welcomed into the system naturally (-via-family businesses, corporate connections or college grants) so that subsequently the folks like us who are still seated at the low end of the see saw still gets disregarded. Everybody considered as a minority knows their own race will empathize and hire them even when they can barely afford to. Blacks are the only idiots who as a race won't help each other "over" helping someone else but we as Crips most certainly will stand up and stay down for our folks no matter what it might look like to the civilian public cuz only we know how hard it is and how dirty its been down here at the ground level of this seesaw system. After all these years, American democracy still presses on even pushing up strong & imposing itself on every other nation it possibly can because to a poor, uneducated nation, Capitalism is so wonderful. Even our Cuban cousins genuinely believe that having the right to capitalize off of someone else, having the right to be a glutton and having the right to prosper is the right system to migrate to but we told them and we swore it on Crip that we do everything to the left becuz the system just ain't right! There are several secret "P's" that are everywhere, secret "perks" and "pointers" go to the "selected" meanwhile we get the secret "Pitfalls" and "Penal codes" and these four (4) P's change the whole landscape of the game in a significant way. Politicians codify the system in a word that goes over most folks' heads, they call it the "Life boat" doctrine: Metaphorically its as if each rich nation or nationality is adrift with no land in sight and the first threat to each lifeboat's national security is its population. The rich have agreed to uphold all their ethical and moral obligations by tossing into the ocean several goodies and medical supplies for the sinking, drowning, starving and overcrowded lifeboats to fish in and survive on. The rich have also tolerated an occasional stow away who'd abandoned his or her own folks lifeboat and swam (pleadingly) to them but their "tough decision" responsibility is to ration properly for to be too generous would only cause sure disaster as (1) the overcrowded poor lifeboats would only increase in population/hardships if their resources were increased and (2) the resources of the rich-slow breeding lifeboats would be depleted amounting to irresponsible suicide. The system as a lifeboat, a seesaw or an animal kingdom is all the same to us because in every scenario we've been relegated to sit at the bottom but we just wouldn't comply. We're disregarded by design, misrepresented by our own and misunderstood. Finally all our faculties are excellent and our disciplines evolved and have excelled. Everything we say and do we shall highly regard just as confidently as white folks who crown each other as Kings and Masters, as the most intelligent or the most beautiful etc, etc... because we've done everything better that every other people have done plus we still stand: Loved by few, hated by many, Respected by All!!!

V. Common Faults

<u>Common faults</u>. We as folks of color do have flaws and faults that hinder our progress as a community raised infantry and perhaps chief among these faults stands our egos.

Ego is one's sense of self as distinguished from others; our own awareness or human consciousness. In this basic capacity, "ego" is not yet a fault, matter of fact, it becomes the inspiration and essence of what gives us pride, making us distinctly confident. However, ego rests on a slippery slope so that once its destabilized, ego slides down into egotism making one egocentric then you get an "inflated" ego that ultimately proves to be a real "ego-problem" then you wake up to find that you've become a fuccin' ego maniac that's bound to get crushed by the cadré. So, our "sense of self" is standard and honorable until you become "overly concerned" with yourself, that's when you check your ego otherwise you'll gradually develop an "exaggerated" sense of self and that immediately becomes "self obsession" that a person will fiercely protect and defend even to the death and destruction of anyone and anything because by then one will have adopted their own paranoid version of "self preservation!" which over rides all honor and morals. This well known flaw is commonly targeted by agents and officers trained on how to exploit it so that most snitches walk away feeling vindicated and relieved for having done the right thing which was to "save yourself" i.e. look out for number one because nobody else will, right? Dishonor before death.

Having a big ego isn't an ego problem until it becomes overly concerned with self or develops the "exaggerated" sense of self; for, where would today's arts and sports be without our enormous swag taking everything to higher levels... slam-dunking 360's in a game originally designed for a person to merely shoot a basketball through the hoops, dancing, painting, boxing, singing and rapping with such a sense of self-confidence the world would otherwise have never known. We've enhanced everything we've touched although we're aware that owning such pride threatens the mainstream we don't stop. They say Mexicans introduced the low rider fad and we agree but it was us who then turned it into a phenomenon by wanting them to hop and pose on three wheels, dancing our Crip walk dance to the enhanced volumes of earth shaking music. Our girls enhanced the way tennis on the women's side was played, hair, nails and fashion would be worn and so on. Our actors, writers and producers have sprinkled the world with small glimpses of our daily slangs in those ghetto streets. Islands and third world countries. Everything that was bland is in jeopardy of encountering flavor so it should've been no shock how things changed once we were introduced to the drug game, the war game, the obtaining treasures of jewelry gave then finally the social-political game which now because we got game, informs us to temper our "all out" violent cut throats for territory game. We still have the big egos and elite cadré mannerisms but our discipline and education now reminds us not to "over exaggerate" that sense of self and become a maniac. By all means we shall continue to Love, Honor and cherish ourselves but at the same time be mentally sober enough to remember who "Self" actually is in this underworld capacity. This is critical because for Us, The C-Nation, The boys in Royal Blue, we as a "self" are a great many. Self is all of us together and none of us alone. We love and hate as One, we Live and die as One! So then, we must Love our whole Self, for our whole Life, with our whole Loyalty, period! For example; naturally everyone won't always be best of friends with everyone so feuds within the family will occur however, these are those key moments where egos play pro (professional) or where "Ego problems" will show. We are duty-bound to protect and promote the family's functionalism at all costs so we have to always be paying attention that none of our actions or our inactions are found to be the cause of a disruption in the machine's forward motion, as obviously dysfunctionalism is dishonor to the code. It takes a hell of alot of discipline to check our own egos but to whom much is given, much is required, so all that we are, then requires, all the more we must do! e.g. The homie Reese and lil Ice-man brawls violently in the street until finally we separate the two, they must go cool off somewhere, one man may need some days or weeks while another may only require a few seconds or a moment but either way they know we're fam-bam so if an outsider tries to attack one of them in front of the other or even tries to stir up plots against the other assuming they are now adversaries, both men immediately sticking to the script shall flip and flash on that outsider. Prison guards have reported these type of puzzling dynamics for decades. A yard full of seemingly divided "selves" merge into one when a "one" of theirs is dishonored or their Blue flag allegiance is being challenged. The same high standards apply to the females too. e.g. A crew of Criplettes arrive early to help liven up a neighborhood party then, well into the wee hours, another crew of homegirls arrive competitively stealing all the homies attention and thereby causing hostilities between the two but when a crew of civilian females clash with either crew of our seemingly adversarial homegirls, they immediately put their own differences to the side and fiercely support each other's "self" like its their own even cuz it actually is. This is called "self" discipline, ego-discipline in honor of Love, in Honor of Life, in honor of Loyalty! So... when all the civilian world's slick little slogans say: "Just do You!"; "You are all that you got!", "I ride solo!", "Im just doing Me!", "At the end of the day, all that really matters is...Me, Myself and I!", "I am just Me!", "I don't care about nobody but numero Uno!" etc... just smile at their forehead as if you can see their peanut sized brains straight through their skulls then pity the fools! No one or nothing can function alone or in a "self' capacity. Ivy League graduates just allow the lesser to feel "self" righteous in these chants. Truth is... Capitalism and functionalism depends on idiots and all the lesser-minds to believe they know whats going on, otherwise they'd keep searching. There is only two occupations in the real world scheme: The providers and the consumers! Then there are three types of people-personalities: Those who make things happen, those who watch things happening and those who just don't know what is happening. In order to MAKE things happen, you've got to be in on a function of some kind. So the very same person who says they are just doing their own thang is usually unaware they are in some role at their job, being loyal and obedient to whatever functionalism some Ivy League C.E.O. has them serving. Everyone and Everything functions in a cycle of some kind to serve some sort at Multi-Million and Billion dollar corporations or Industry but us and only us alone are involved in contributing to our own Legacy. We live and we die in this eternal Crip matrix where our deeds matter, our contributions are on eternal file, our names become that of legends and ultimately we live on in the hearts and minds of the cadre and community we served meanwhile, the clown who worked loyal till he died for proctors and gamblers (so deliberate misspelling!) shall be remembered by no one and is building a legacy of nothingness. On his tombstone there is no adorations from that job he served, only one name, only one forgotten dead ego, only one lovely single SELF! dishonorably discharged and gone... No Crip's ego should be his or her own undoing so check your "self" before you wreck your..."self"!!!

Another common fault or flaw we must grapple with is called: "Emotions!"

Emotions - are the list of intense feelings we have that flaw us whenever we allow them into our personal space. The most controversial truth that we can ever own is the knowledge and awareness that emotion is a melanin carried affliction. It's controversial because all the people loaded with the highest quantity of the stuff is already (Metaphorically) cemented into the basement floors and lowest level walls of all the world's tallest skyscrapers. It would be utter madness to attempt to right certain wrongs, some things simply can never be undone so it would be irresponsible to even try. In total honor and respect for these holy Scriptures I shall put forth the supporting evidence then let Real eyes. Realize, Real Lies. For hundreds and hundreds of years we've succumbed to emotions. For example: The media tells us (subliminally) to hate the kid who killed another kid because he's a thug-gang member meanwhile we'll empathize with the sad life story of the white kid who tried to kill, bury alive a whole bus full of school children. Or... we should hate Kardashian (all she ever did was fall in love with black love) but love Paula Dean who made an apology for hate.

Emotions without question is one of the most common flaws and faults that we'll face in the underworld. Emotions obviously are the essential characteristics that separates and distinguishes human beings from all other living organisms and things but you'll easily notice that no one is ever taught how to unlock the secret code and master our emotions. This is vital information that the Crip Nation must know and know it well because whenever we slip and allow our emotions to trip, its possible and probable that somebody might wind up getting flipped! With such great power comes great responsibility and so, because the Cadres are so diverse and our influences have spread so vastly across the planet, it is the duty of us evolved cousins to share our intell especially on a matter as critical such as this.

There are a number specific emotions everyone obviously shall encounter on a more regular and constant basis and in these routine encounters, just knowing or being aware aint gonna be the factor that makes the difference for us. When we're pissed off or we're sad we know damn well how we're feeling. The secret technique to controlling and tempering these feelings is this: Know the tiers! We've discovered that most emotions have 2 to 3 different tiers; different levels of intensity that they manifest themselves on. This is extremely useful information because when one occurs, we now have the genius to check and correct ourselves or remind a loved one that is caught up in one emotion or another to check and correct his or herself and to dial down from whatever tier they are. For example: A loved one has died, we notice and respect that folk must grieve so the first tier is obvious: "Sadness". After a reasonable amount of time, sadness can become "depression" which is its natural second tier. "Depression" unchecked can and will develop into despondency which is its natural third tier. These very natural, gradual stages can and will often occur when we ourselves don't notice our own emotional change and then most certainly when the Crip Community around us is derelict in duty and nobody notices and checks it for us. Sadness is cool and expected under its given circumstance but tier two "depression" is when that sadness is harming our loved ones or ourselves with inactivity, psychological difficulty and lowered spirits. This is classic disrespect to the Crip Mind, Body and Soul royalty. Then the third tier is "Despondency", where a Crips has actually fallen so low that there are emotions of "hopelessness, discouragement and even disheartened feelings of resignation. This is not just beyond cool but actually becomes a real serious security issue for the whole community. It absolutely is our responsibility to protect ourselves and each other which is one in the same because one can't protect himself or herself without protecting everyone around us so that everyone connected to the cadre is secured and strong.

TIERS OF EMOTIONS

First Tier	Second Tier	Third Tier
Annoy = To disturb or Upset. Frustration = an induced feeling of dissatisfaction or insecurity Disappointment = the feeling of unfulfilled expectations	Angry = emotional excitement that's induced by intense displeasure. Pissed off = outwardly heated: or visibly mad to the level where its apparent.	Rage = blindly furious; violent and uncontrolled anger where nothing matters.
Sadness = sorrow; mournful; or grieving.	Depression = lowered spirits; A psychological disorder that also can reduce the appetite and physical activity.	Despondence = Hopelessness, discouraged; resigned. (psychologically & physically)
Like = is to casually prefer; enjoy.	Love = Strong affection; Devotion.	Adore = extreme fondness; worship.
Guarded = Watchful; Alert.	Cautious = Prudent forethought to minimize risk.	Paranoia = Delusions usually marked by irrational suspicions.
Cool = calmly happily composed feeling. Happy = fortunate; pleased; cheerful.	Joyful = experiencing pleasure and delight.	Ecstatic = extreme emotional excitement. (Ecstasy)
Concern – An anxious uneasiness. A casual awareness	Fear = A strong emotional awareness of danger (i.e. Healthy fear)	Cowardice = shrinking in the face of fear (self preservation).
Confidence = Trust; reliance; self-assurance; Boldness.	Pride = Justifiable self respect. Self regard.	Arrogance = Offensively exaggerated sense of self-importance.
Desire = To strongly wish for; long or hope for	Jealousy = Rival or suspicious of another for having advantages. Drive = Motivation to achieve desires.	Envy = Painful resentment/awareness of another's advantages. Greed = selfish desire beyond reason.

Crip-Down = A homie who is always in uniform (Wearing Blue) and representing the Cadré well.	Crip-Crazy = A homie who is always speaking, thinking and projecting Crip in whatever gear he/she wears.	Cripped Out = A homie who shows little regard for anyone or anything and Crips dysfunctionally.

These tiers of emotions are just a few notable examples of how they differ in their early stages and then gradually their characteristics turn more intense and often irrational. Emotions have always had an esoteric pattern, a pattern that would only be understood by a select few, however... in this era of blue enlightenment it is the Crips that are the select few who shall understand and even master all of our emotions.

First of all we did the research and discovered that the melanin in our bodies circulates in our brains and is responsible for the darkness of our skin just as it colors the leaves, flowers and grass and is a conductor for human emotions. Ultimately this was a devastating revelation for us to process, this was an actuality that we didn't want to see or hear cause it virtually tells us why people of color are inferior and easy to deceive then conquer. We are a people who can easily be pushed onto third tiers in the emotions context and most emotions become irrational on the third tier and don't stand a chance against folks who are remaining functional and rational because they are on a less intense tier. For example... It begins in grade school where children of all races learn about slavery, the black children will internalize a second or third tier anger, concern or sadness which psychologically cripples their rational ability to process information in school, meanwhile... the white child experiences first tier emotions so their anger isn't rage but merely disappointment in their forefathers for annihilating these helpless, nice people. They experience concern in the casual awareness sense instead of the type of second or third tier emotional awareness which reduces a lot of Blacks to a depressed or discouraged coward in racial matters. Most blacks still deny or look away from racisms or in most cases as T.V. personalities and politicians they'll minimize it and allow it to fade away. Another example which is common is how white folks economically and socially may experience first tier "Desires" or be a bit "Guarded" until their social circle becomes more transparent while we jump higher on the emotional tier and instead of having a functional and rational desire economically, we're experiencing greed and envy that causes us to murder each other for crumbs then feel like its justified in the name of survival and hunger. Socially we jump from the first tier of just being emotionally alert and watchful and find ourselves in every community as being irrationally suspicious and paranoid of one another which is a reason why we blow each other away in the blink of an eye. White folks dealing with thirty times the amount of money we're dealing with and they don't even bother packing a pistol and yet we can do no moving unless we got bullet proof vests, a pistol with extra clips and an entourage of rip-riders posted up at the ready. We're all too third tier and irrational in matters that involve emotions but from now on, for those of us stickin' to the Script, we are functioning on that superior level. Mastering our emotions means we will deport ourselves more calm and calculatingly, generally functioning on first tier emotions with second tier potentiality. Third tier emotions will usually be the ones we'll have to make amends for and/or apologize to the cadré for when we hit those extremes.

A multi-millionaire was quoted as saying: "To prosper, I didn't set out believing that I was the smartest man in the world but I did understand that I would have to eventually study their ways and copy some of the smartest!"

In context, this means that we've gotta work hard to block out and master these emotions we are saddled with. White folks have protocols and first tier emotions. Even the concept of love is a fairly new characteristic fused into their marriages and procreations.

Their whole measure of companionship even today is still largely promised on Social protocols saying: blue eyes, blond hair, green eyes with red hair equals attractiveness. And then the Economic protocols of: Blue blooded, prestigious family line, a rich history and/or a promising future. All this is first tier with the potential to grow into second tier affections but there are a countless amount of pro athletes and black businessmen who will tell you that those cold blue eyes can very easily just wake up and decide to cut it all in half and go. There is no logic and reasonableness that compels them to marry or procreate with a poor person, there is no flow of melanin, virtually there is no love, just pragmatic instincts. This is the discipline we must study and acquire. In even the most catastrophic of circumstances the white men will display their "Moosh-mouth" where both top and bottom lips are tightly rolled inward so that their face looks mushed or where the women will cover her mouth with the classic trembling hand (or hands to the mouth and then stacked over her heart) in solemn disbelief. As Crips we've gotta' recognize how advantageous emotional protocols are especially in those situations where we would generally explode in rage. The evolved Crip, knowing to collect himself and stick to the Script can be told that his car just got fired-bombed or his home just got shot at and he'll deport himself in such a calm and collected way that the perpetrators will tremble wondering what manner of man or Criplette is this. Shouting and fussing is reserved for loved ones whom we deem worthy of our emotions but even then it should be tempered. Furthermore there are all types of things that occur daily which we must respond to and personalities we must identify, for example:

TIERS of Occurrences and Personalities

First Tier	Second Tier	Third Tier
<u>Crip Sex</u> = Intercourse.	<u>Crip Passion</u> = hood promiscuity.	<u>Nymphomania</u> = Sex addict.
<u>Discussions</u> = To talk about a matter together thoughtfully.	<u>Debating</u> = To consider both sides in a structured format. (Blue Room).	<u>Arguing</u> = Disputing with words and tone but not listening to each other.
<u>Crip Business</u> = Matters which require discreteness; on the low.	<u>Confidential</u> = Need to know (N.T.K.) information.	<u>The Blue Code</u> = Silence in search/suspicion of a breech.
<u>A kick back</u> = a small gathering (usually intimate couples or a crew).	<u>A Party</u> = A hood gathering a celebration open to all homies.	<u>A Function</u> = A mega gathering usually involving several hoods.
<u>Trustworthy smart</u> = A homie with honor and no insecurities about following a plan exactly.	<u>Specialty Intelligence</u> = A homie who knows the outs and ins of a particular craft; a specialist.	<u>Certifiable Mastermind</u> = A homie who is a specialist in at least "3" correlating Faculty disciplines.

<u>Entertaining</u> = A homie who is often funny or comical to enjoy.	<u>Jokester</u> = A homie that clowns all the time; enjoys the attention.	<u>Narcissism</u> = A jokester homie who is obsessed with having the attention, even breaking protocols.
<u>A Loc</u> = A homie who is crazy in a fun or loyal way that everyone can relate to.	<u>A Nut</u> = A homie who is just "burnt out" in the crazy cousin way but also a bit "off", yet still can be reined in and loved.	<u>A Fool</u> = A homie who isn't receptive to Crip protocols or counseling. Is funny-sad and determined to wreck; a stupid fool.
<u>A Mac</u> = A homie with the verbal gift of gab and usually the physical to back it up.	<u>A Player</u> = A homie with the physical gift of satisfying and of juggling multiple relationships.	<u>A Pimp</u> = A homie with the verbal gift of persuasion and usually the physical to back it up.
<u>A True Blue</u> = A rip rider who reps the hood with Love, Life and Loyalty.	<u>A Hood-Star</u> = A Crip rider who is notorious for his displays of Love, Life and Loyalty.	<u>A Hot Mess</u> = A homie with a hot temper who claims his/her own uniqueness as their reasoning.

Most of these occurrences and personalities are so regular and common that we've all either been on most of the levels/tiers at some point or we've witnessed a homie on one of those irrational levels/third tiers where an emotion or a personality went too extreme or went in way too hard and something went wrong maybe somebody even wrecked. As evolved-elite loved ones we're laying out our high expectations of one another, we're in effect, putting everybody on notice that our lives are valuable, too valuable to be destroyed or denied just because of someone else's mistake or blooper. From now on folks had better be sticking to the script so that if something goes wrong they will have some bit of protection while those who are doing and come to the table with an "Oops, Im sorry" type defense, there is none! The first tier conduct is standard Crip excellence, the second tier is usually an enhanced level of excellence and the third tier is often the overblown, irrational displays of what coulda', woulda', shoulda' been excellence yet becomes a liability and possibly a transgression. Our goal, our duty and commitment is Excellence and we aint taking no shorts!

Another common fault we suffer from is "unconscious ambushing".

We often unconsciously ambush our own loved ones by saying "yes" when we wanted to say "no!". When we extend ourselves beyond what is comfortable to us and agonize ourselves for a loved one, actually we're harboring emotions that will eventually come out. Playing cool with things that we are not genuinely cool with only becomes a source of penned up frustrations. This is an ambush waiting to happen because: #1. The particular loved one(s) you bless is certainly going to feel welcomed to return and impose on you again or allow those same circumstances to be re-visited upon you again and causing that same agony, discomfort or frustration you felt before to hit you again. #2. The feeling you penned up will suddenly be compounded with more of the same and a release will at some point occur. This frustration being a sort of hair-pin-trigger will fire off or explode disproportionately upon a loved one and it will have been your bad for not making them aware of how you really felt the first and second time it happened.

Unconscious Ambushes can show up in so many different forms, far too many to be categorically spelled out in these scriptures but one key to keep in mind if you want to identify this common butt is to re evaluate and examine arguments and disputes that occur between those you care about or who you know cared about you. More often than not these types of disputes & feuds are more vicious and volatile and can go unresolved because no one is actually at fault but both will have been wronged by the other. The ambusher will have been over used or abused of his or her own kindness while the other will have been attacked with an explosion of hostility or sarcasm by a one who they genuinely believed was cool with their arrangement i.e. Ambushed! So then, we would do well to learn to master such ambushings on both ends so that if and when you are the ambusher or the ambushee you'll know its just a common flaw, a fault that should not be able to prevail over Love, certainly not Crip Love, Crip Life or Crip Loyalty! These are common faults because they are real occurrences that take place amongst the masses. We need not deny or try to explain away our common faults because what's more important now is that we know them and change the way we respond to them on a regular basis. Throughout the Nation we've got a ton of different issues that frustrate and pressure us and the way we respond to a loved one's or even a second cousins issues will decide a lot of Love, possible lives and future Loyalty. What's most disturbing about this particular flaw is not just that it is so very common within the cadre but more so because its done "unconsciously" meaning that you nor I can imagine at all that we're ambushing someone that we love and care for but right now at this moment we certainly are. What's saddest about the flaws that plagues us most, not just as The Nation but particularly as black folks world wide is our ignorance (the state of unawareness; not knowing) not regarding academic matters but our genuine ignorance about what Love really is when its coming from society and what Love is not! A key pearl of wisdom explains that the total opposite of love is not "hate" but its actually "Indifference". Black folks on every continent has this desperate and deep desire to be embraced by society so much so that they scoff at each other then the lighter shaded blacks, they distance themselves from their darker shaded kind and cling to fabricated race titles and cultures ignorantly believing this is their bridge to societal love and prosperity.

Indifference is subtle but catastrophic to a people so visceral about exchanging love with everyone, so passionate about loving people of all races and in our state of rejection we turn on one another while shouting out "I don't give a f**k!", & "It's no big deal!" because "Love don't Love Nobody!". Well for our Cadré this ignorance has got to end. "Real" love does love somebody even as do hate. We fight and war in the name of so called hate, we tattoo each other's monikers or neighborhoods on our bodies (and in our hearts) and then cross it out with an "ex" and vow to hate them forever but their legacy is now living on in and through us. We disregard real life history only to worship and covet the history and legacy we are told to memorialize by society and the media but in truth, those whom we deem our hated adversaries are actually the counterpart of our wholeness. The Yin to our Yang, etc... Disregard is a nasty, demonic tool which we must never use on one another nor shall we weaponize it in an irresponsible way. We need our polar opposites beside us as our demarcation line in history and to disregard a people, place, culture or Crip we don't like often costs us part of our own rich history in the process. Legacies usually have to have both the positive and the negative; arriving at a great destination is only astonishing if there's some great journey one had to traverse inorder to get there so if we were to be flippant (disregarding the journey) and claim we only came here from next door, yes we may have successfully erased that journey we despise but also we've devalued and dishonored the meritorious process it took us to arrive there. Legacies require balance for example, Rwanda has a rich history that cant be recognized unless the Hutus and the Watutsis are equally acknowledged. What kind of history could chronicle the Serbians without the balance of the Croatian portion, who has heard of the vice lords without knowing they exist beside the Disciples, who has knowledge of the bloods without knowing they are stalked by the Crips. This is our reality, this is our True histories and within the pages of history glows our legacy and that which makes up our legacy shall be disregarded by no man or woman.

Now, of course in the smaller more local context we disregard each other so casually and commonly completely unaware of what a transgression it is against the cadre. The C-Nation's legacy and ourselves.

To truly understand how serious of a transgression this local disregard is, one must first truly understand how serious life and legacy is. Genesis 12:2-3 "I will make you a great Nation; I will bless you and make your name great; and you shall be a blessing. I will bless those who bless you and I will curse him who curses you; And in you All the families of the earth shall be blessed." It is a guarded fact that God crafted and designed human life to have a purpose, to make an impact that lasts beyond his or her designated time and this, in a word, is called: Legacy! Therefore to exist and not impact nothing or leave no lasting legacy actually offends the Creator and proclaims that of all He Created, you were the waste. Its no coincidence nor is it ironic that all our captors: English slave traders, Portuguese slave traders and Spaniard slave traders all shared a fervent belief in their Holy Bible where the specific parable by the Lord himself about the kingdom of heaven says: three servants are given talents as their precious Jewels. One servant gets five and invests them, one servant is given two talents yet he invests them while the third servant who only had one talent hid his in the ground until the Lord's return. The moral goes, the Lord was only pleased with those two servants who invested what talents they had but for that poorest servant who hid his talents that they had no impact on nothing at all, the Lord called him "wicked and lazy", took the one talent and gave it to him with the most and said to the one "cast the unprofitable servant into the outer darkness. There will be weeping and gnashing of teeth". (Matthew 25:14-30). So then all our captors had the right idea even as did Abraham in Genesis, we must pursue and protect our legacy which ultimately shall be our Eternal life and to live in a fashion that disregards our legacy is in effect you killing our whole life. One must never forget this. Life and living is all about Legacy!

Now... in common everyday life, all throughout the cadré we tend to look at each other with such disregard to where we're often heard saying things to each other like: "boy, who you think you are?" or "girl, you aint all that!" or... "he ain't shit!" or... "dat' punk bitch is a ho!" well sometimes we fuss and fight all in fun but one must beware because gradually folks begin to believe whats being heard and said. One pearl of wisdom forewarns us that: "familiarity breeds contempt." So, the more we feel we know each other, the less we tend to respect and fear them. Our thoughts become our words, our words become our actions, our actions then become our habits and naturally now our habits become our character which in all fairness is essentially our life. The formula for dissolving all these actions and unlearning all these habits of disregard for one another is this:

The exercise of reality and deductive reasoning by way of a series of questions we shall ask ourselves. (1) Is this an instance where my familiarity is breeding such contempt that it's blocking out merit? (2) Is this an emotional reaction/response to something said or done? (3) Is this my best pragmatic reaction/response to something said or done.

First and foremost we as this community raised infantry must face the real fact that we've all got a lot more merit than any civilians we can picture simply because we've all chosen Love, Life and Loyalty! We've taken the Oath, we've all got the same honorable family values and exhibited the courage to risk death for our Legacy rather than long life as just a consumer cowardly shrinking in the face of adversity. Even the least among us has this great amount of Merit glowing in and around him or her and therefore question #1. asks if it's our own over familiarity with one-another that is blinding us and blocking us from regarding the merit every Crip already possesses. This is a very common fault and certainly a very important question one must explore whenever one is at odds with a cousin all while having such huge respect and admiration for our favorite celebrity.

Secondly, we must identify immediately if we are feeling a strong emotion (rage, sadness, jealousy, etc...) causing us to feel dismissive and to disregard a cousin. As humans we simply MUST understand what our strengths are and what our weaknesses are and accept that often we are emotional. "For we all stumble in many things. If anyone does not stumble in word(s) he is a perfect man, able also to bridle the whole body." (James 3:2) So then, what other than emotions can cause us to beef with our own loved ones and carry out eternal war campaigns that produce no financial gains nor makes our community any safer...? "Emotions!" There are a number emotions that can't all be laid out here but that we all can testify to. "Where do wars and fights come from among you? Do they not come from our desires for pleasure that war in your members?" (James 4:1) Never function on Emotions.

Third and finally we must determine what would be the pragmatic thing to do, almost robotic in the sense that emotions are completely out of play and the only concern is the functionalism. Being pragmatic requires us to look no further than to whatever keeps the Cadre moving, functioning efficiently. Pragmatism boggles the minds of almost everyone except the highly educated folks, the Ivy Leaguers who can operate on a patient and save the life of an individual who was just shot while trying to kill him. Or the racist judge who can "sometimes" acquit the black defendant. The central objective we must all learn to hold fast to is the continued function of the cadré machine and whenever we disregard or fail to honor even with a healthy tinge of far or atleast caution, a Crip then we are in effect derailing the moving train function our fore runners already died for. Disregard being the opposite of Love is basically just a subtle form of dishonor and even disrespect. It's already established that as family members, each and everyone of us have merit. So, in context, to speak to an Italian Mafioso with more respect and regard than you would to a Crip who exists in a daily war, who kills and dies for your family values and who even carries within his or her memory bank episodes of "your" legacy, is completely absurd, nonetheless, it is extremely common. It's a common fault of one which keeps the concrete splattered with blue blood, death and betrayals as lessons of what the meritorious do when they are disregarded. At some point we've gotta be pragmatic and view the evidence right in front of us which tells us all that we're all some very dangerous, very deadly sons of bitches. At some point we've got to believe also that most of us aren't cowards scared to die! It's foolish to continue, generation after generation proving to each other almost like a silly cartoon... "fool,

I ain't scared to die!" then... "Oh, yea, well I ain't afraid to kill yo' ass!" and then boom bam next! "Cuz, I aint no punk!" then... "Oh yeah? Well I aint no punk either so we gonna see who's the punk!" and then Boom, bam! Two of our soldiers dead proving they wasn't no punks. Meanwhile some of these weenie ass actors and fake rappers will put together a made up story and have us worship their words more than each others who we know for sure is right here deep in the trenches beside us. This is foolish disregard! We gotta' check our familiarity at critical times of dispute where our emotions kick in and tell us not to give a fuck because ain't nothing honorable about dying out of line, dying off duty, dying on a dare to prove that death don't kill. Honor is in sticking to the Script and history will echo legacies for the meritorious who evolves and promotes the functioning system we all depend on.

Our females must not be disregarded either because every criplette wears a crown of merit that far out shines any fake Hollywood crowns. We commonly disregard and take for granted her generosity in yielding her weapons of war to us, all over us, in the heat of ghetto passions and lust even without the costly price of death lingering nearby as it would if we were her marked target. Instead we fall from between her wings, thoroughly drained, only to call her a hoodrat, punk bitch or a ho. All this while we praise and lust over the actresses and swimsuit models that have no merits nor weapons of war or any of our family values but cuz she's unfamiliar to us, we respect and perhaps even love these females who slut their way through Hollywood and modeling projects randomly in pursuit of anything they can get but nothing in particular. Females that have no loyalties to nothing but their own vanities and perceptions of fame, these are they whom all our athletes marry and give kids to.

Disregard is merely a symptom that can be seen systematically emitting from a society functioning in a psychopathic capacity. The lack of feelings of guilt is usually defined by disregard which is usually perpetrated and qualified by the mass media thereby making it a society's norm. Then to dare to speak out against a society's normal behavior is obviously social suicide. It's no wonder news anchors, politicians, business moguls and celebrities all will sit tight-lipped and smile as white folks hot topics will be to publicize black icons on their actual day of death in the most deplorable fashion. Any accusations and dirty mishaps a dead black person can be loosely tied to will instantly become the discussion of the day as they are being laid to rest and the smartest, most dedicated black socialites will eagerly join in on this psychopathic disregard because they know that their brand as a professional will be propelled instantly to higher echelons of social trust. Ultimately to be in any position where you are heard by or known to the masses means you have at some point satisfied the quiet prerequisites of the psychopaths in control, at some point you lost your way and at some point you really began to believe the verbal hype which uses reason to quality and explain away the deeds and behaviors a psychopathic society practices and perfects as its norms. This psychopathic behavior has been around so long and has become so resilient to scrutiny that there are automated safeguards that kick in to protect it. e.g. for people of color (black, yellow or brown) who dares to pick history apart they will immediately be classified as hate-provocateurs, mongers or sympathizers; for white people who dare to take bold stands, they are immediately classified as "apologist" suffering from "white guilt" and are then socially damaged themselves, meanwhile, in between these two ostracized voices of dissent lands the seemingly fair voice of reason which cites the law known as "Natural selection" that is often articulated by societies, politicians, etc... (of every race) whom have pragmatically concluded that the down-trodden and disregarded victims of our great society merely needs education, motivation and dedication and one day they too can win. This is an ancient tactic known as the: Ad Hominem technique as it shifts the argument to focus on the human "personally" instead of the issue professionally and no anchor, politician or celebrity ever wants that type of cloud of scrutiny hovering over their heads. It's basically up to us, the actual folks being so shrewdly disregarded to learn to just highly regard ourselves. It simply just makes sense for folks like us stuck in a society founded by conquerors and master architects of deception to change course, it just makes more sense for folks like us stuck in a society where capitalizing upon others so thoroughly is the way the system works and where we find ourselves as the main course dish being fed so thoroughly into this system, it more than just makes sense, it becomes our duty even that we must finally unlearn all the ideas and poisonous protocols this system has subliminally bred into us through these norms of such a society. We must change course by changing our thinking (our regard for one another) which will ultimately change our fate. Our late Chairman, Stanley Tookie Williams asked for Redemption to the true "Redemption Song":.None but ourselves can free our minds... How long can they kill our prophets and we just stand around and look, some say it's just a prophecy we got to fulfill the Book...Wont you help me sing this song of freedom, cuz all I ever have is Redemption Songs..."

-Bob Marley (Redemption Song)

From day to day, month to month and year to year we must deliberately and excellently go an extra mile inorder to give a homeboy or homegirl some sort of high regard. Be it with words to or about him or her in front of civilians or in deeds to or for him or her in the form of making him or her shine in front of the civilian world, we each are duty bound to pay forward some solid portions of Crip-Regards e.g. on certain school days, a bunch of homies caravan up to the young locs school precisely as the last bell rings, hitting our switches on the low riders and giving a show until all our young locs are rounded up and acknowledged or... on certain weekends a bunch of homies caravan up to all the hair and nails salons where groups of homegirls are congregated waiting to get fly or find them feeling bored at the county building in long lines waiting for their checks. At some point everybody that's true blue is gonna be regarded while the iconic celebrities we all know and love are ignored and often disregarded as they stroll down such unroyal carpets at the Awards shows pining for the attention they all rightly deserve but will never get from this cold society already pre designed to disregard them.

It saddens us to see our artists and athletes attacked so viciously from every side whenever a foul comment or mistake is made on their parts meanwhile when something is done or said on the part of any other race, blacks are the first to help explain it away. As Crips we've been disregarded by all the black talk shows and white talk shows who both proudly cover the klan's regularly spewing hate. We know the game of disregard and we're not mad at the Oprah's and the Whoopi's who lack understanding of this callous technique, the B.E.T. networks or the magazines that all pretend we don't exist because our pride, our focus and our legacy is bullet proof in our hearts.

Disregard has a lot of dirty dimensions too vast to explore but a final notable is our common disregard for our second cousins and stakeholders. These are those non-Crip parties of paramount importance whose functionality is not at all threatened by our functionality but willingly functions right along with us to both our benefits. This is a complicated reality that everyone is not able to comprehend and therefore by word of the Script we just gotta' blindly accept it and respect it. Second cousins might not have the street-merits which is like interchangeable currency among us from cadré to cadré but their merits are priceless to us in other faculty disciplines.

Our esteemed Treasury team or the Investments and fundraisings team might deem one of these second cousins extremely meritorious and so invaluable to the existence of multipole cadres throughout the whole nation. Your disregard for them in disrespect to them and every one whom might be involved and the only end result for resolve might be to ship out by mail small pieces of your ass to all the different cadrés overseas and whoever in the Nation demands their portion of the transgressor(s)! Second cousins under our Royal blue allegiance shall all be respected and regarded by us just as absolutely as we demand they respect and regard us throughout their ranks. Having, maintaining and mastering the art of "showing" regard is a virtue, it is a particularly moral excellence and a commendable quality which we all must practice to obtain. For those of us who know better, you are herein called to do better and for the homies who don't quite understand how to show regard... to make this simpler, just behave like you see in the godfather and Japanese mafia movies towards one another; Committed to excellence we shall Love with virtue, Live Life with fire and remain Loyal with honor and dignity knowing that the opposite of Love is... disregard.

The Religious and Sociological Politic of Disregard

Religious disregard was originally known as Excommunication and dates back over a thousand years when Catholic Rome remarkably weaponized it to disregard other religions old and new, their own Catholic transgressors then it became so efficient that it even frightened artists, philosophers. Scribes and kings into submission. The Holy Roman church was so bold even to threaten King Henry VIII with this weapon of absolute disregard if he continued to pursue getting a divorce. Ultimately King Henry VIII broke from the Roman Catholic umbrella then formed the Church of England (1535 A.D.) This was known as the "Reformation era" and it wasn't until 1553 Queen Mary I restored Roman Catholicism to England, followed by Queen Elizabeth I 1558 whom restored the Protestant movement (Anglicanism) to the state Church of England, however... even she was also excommunicated later in 1570 A.D. by the Pope as was the faithful Martin Luther in 1520 by Pope Leo X.

The effective weaponization of disregard is absolutely an art and it certainly requires a certain amount of shrewdness and psychopathic populaces. This popular group dynamic is one that is very apparent but forbidden to be addressed because the folks who are guilty of this atrocious behavior are still masters of the art even to this day. Being a psychopath is not only culturally a group dynamic that melanin-deficient people have enjoyed to great success and prosperity but as evidenced by history, psychopathic behavior is hereditary yet we as Crips have no problem treading dangerous waters or on forbidden ground so let's keep it real. Real eyes must Realize the truth from Real lies. A psychopath may seem like an insulting thing to be or for us to call a person but actually its not. Emotions are actually what cripples folks from having the type of ferocity and world dominance that psychopaths enjoy. Being or having these psychopathic genes just means: One who has not lost contact with reality but who engages in abnormally aggressive and seriously irresponsible behavior with little or no feelings of guilt. Plus, this psychopathic behavior must be predominant as an accepted (even sacred) value that a people will protect and defend vigorously. Examples of this are evident throughout history. The little or no guilt white folks must've felt while publicly torturing Jesus Christ to death or their bloody diaspora on each other (dispersing of the Jews), the horrific slaughter of an entire settlement of Danish women, children and old men in England (1002 A.D.), The great Schism (The Split) between the Orthodox and Catholic churches from each other (1054 A.D.) followed by the religious crusades ordered by Pope Urban II to take the holy land from the Muslims (Antioch 1098 A.D. Jerusalem 1099 A.D.) and so many more atrocities that while society welcomed as the Norms throughout the Dark ages, the Medieval ages with Inquisitions, Plagues, Revolts and Slavery laws that bring this psychopathic behavior to today. Here on the 20th anniversary of our L.A. riots which we had to kick off in response to their... abnormally aggressive behavior with little or no feelings of guilt, now again and again a black teenager in Florida is killed freely because he allegedly looked threatening in his hoodie, this time the shooter is even a civilian. There's no feelings of guilt or empathy from the black news anchors or talk show panelist because they know that one should never anger a society of psychopaths however there are a great many of these black anchors and celebrity panelist whom are genuine docile and brainwashed as they are electing to rather show empathy for the poor soldier who was passed up for his promotion and overly deployed into service so he accidentally creeped into the homes of 17 innocent souls and claimed them all (9 kids and infants 6 women and 2 old men) all to quench that same old psychopathic thirst for blood.

Self Projectionism

Self Projection is one of the most common faults among all humans but the spirit of these holy scriptures is not to inspire or prescribe us to simply be mere mortals plagued with these most common faults but rather to be better and to deport ourselves in a higher, more excellent fashion.

Self projection essentially is when a person or group of people attribute their way of thinking, of feeling and/or their personal characteristics onto another man or woman as an accurate assessment or association of what he or she is thinking or feeling or what the subject's unknown characteristics must be.

Self projection answers questions one is too lazy, too incompetent or just too preoccupied to examine thoroughly to answer. This makes the spectrum of self-projection far too common to absolutely purge out from among us, and the fashions in which it takes form are far too vast to herein chronicle totally, however, for the benefit of our advancement and higher learning these scriptures shall provide:

e.g. 1. Three cousins at the L.A.X. airport (two guys and one girl) are flying first class to one of the Caribbean islands for their cadré faculty meeting, they notice on the other side of the terminal a young black man with an elderly white woman and younger latina girl with royal blue hair. All flights are put on a 3-hour delay so the two groups cross paths at a nearby restaurant. They notice each other more than once throughout the course of their dining experience while surveying the exits, the restroom users and the waiters. Be it paranoia or excellent self security, both groups are given to sudden self projections. The young Latina tells the older white woman and younger black man that she believes the three young blacks at the other table might be jackers or assassins following them, then asked if she should call in the heat. The older white woman had also noticed the trio and summarily deduced that they were just three punk kids undeserving of a second thought while their third party (the youngster with the cauliflower ears) assured both females that he could control everything by walking over and asking them a few dumb tourist questions just to get a feel of who they were and what they might be up to. Meanwhile the first three cousins just a few tables away, still watching everything and everyone, now notices the two women and the well-built black man excusing himself from their table and approaching with a focused and deliberate pace. One man thinks he's a mere "wanna-be" Crip possibly about to ask which cadre they are from, while the second man winks at the female travelling with them who immediately stands and moves in front of the approaching young man, shes a highly trained martial artist capable and prepared to cripple or kill him to protect her comrades.

#1. Synopsis: The first three cousins enroute to the islands are faculty members, 2 from the pulse, (their hood's treasury team) and 1 from the squad (their hood's Booting and recruiting team) adequately trained as their protection. The two pulse members are businessmen and store owners more accustomed to seeing lots of people moving about so their self projection produced a normal store-like environment with those type of flags and subliminal alarms needing to be touched off while their female security being more prone to physical combat stood in anticipation of what she naturally projected as a hand to hand combat situation. Likewise among the second group of Crips, the older white woman being a senior member of her cadre's Walkway team (The Travels and Communications team) depends heavily on other folks projections of her all around the world but being burdened by her own self projections only saw the three younger Crips on the opposite side as mere punks. Her young female comrade representing their heat team only projected a possible need for more heat (i.e. gunplay) and their male comrade with the cauliflower ears being a member of their cadre's Squad team (and a professional Mixed Martial Arts fighter) self projected an easy combat situation. All six Crips were wrong.

Self projection is a way of life for mere mortals, however... for us sticking to the Script we've certainly gotta' put to use our great advantage. Peep game!

e.g. #2. Very wealthy cousins (Athletes, Hustlers, Businessmen, Entertainers and Models) often tend to project the importance of money and fame because in their minds as told in their circles: "everybody got they hands out!" or "Money doesn't change you, money will change the people around you!" such clichés that feed into the self projections that'll define how our wealthy cousins begin to see us. Obviously most of our Black and Latino Crips with major money will fall in deep love with someone white and only return to us in those hood slums once everything is all gone because we're all that's left standing.

Self projections are responsible for absolutely every emotion that we feel because our "feeling it" by definition is rooted and grounded in what we believe.

e.g. #3. We project from the data in our own minds that, to allow these fools to get away with what they did: 'is foul', it's disrespectful and it says we are cowards. That alone makes it unthinkable to let them get away with it no matter what "it" may entail. This train of thought is also reasoned and reinforced by our own opinion of what defines something foul, disrespectful or cowardice as well, it's mostly relative.

e.g. #4. Two Crips have sex, a third Crip perceives their tryst highly disrespectful because of his own self projection from what he believes in his heart is disrespectful which he himself never, ever would have done to that homegirl he lusted and homeboy he trusted. These inner beliefs often stem from one's youth and are difficult to find, and even more difficult to root out. Self projections usually represent the deepest core of an individual so much so that men and women have killed themselves and others over what they are perceiving/projecting from within their minds, so, these matters are to be handled thoughtfully and delicately.

Self projections can and will be weaponized either for you or against you even as Crips. Our empathy is so raw and hyper sensitive that we often hurt and compromise in the face of our own periods of supremacy. This especially applies to any African Americans or blacks descending from the cruelty of slavery. Their self projections of cruelty being done to their forefathers and mothers will always halt these blacks from ever being dominant or dictators over non-black people and thus they always relinquish the power they get and only weaponized it against their own kind in a sort of self loathing-self projection of believing themselves unworthy to rule. These are a few of the most common precursor "trains-of-thought" to watch out for:

(1) Who do you think You are? (2) You ain't nobody! (3) "You're trying to act like you are All that!" (4) She think she the shit! (5) "You ain't running shit but your mouth" Self projections are at work when they become a person's pattern/belief system

e.g. #5. The one waving constant doubts about their hood's ability to be high-tech an deathly serious is speaking from his or her own inner feelings of doubt, sometimes reassurance can cure their self projections of doubt. Those beliefs must change! Its all about mind over matter so then... if you dont mind, it dont matter! "Minds of steel."!

Faulty Framing

Faulty Framing is not just another one of the most common faults we have but this (when used craftily) has proven throughout history to be the single most effective weapon in the arts of war practiced by some of the greatest tacticians and Generals ever. Framing in the social context is just a metaphor describing the outline or shaping of a broad viewpoint, topic or public argument. Framing sets the perimeter on all sides and almost like a cookie-cutter slammed down on a flat layer of cookie dough, it creates these boundaries within its frame and virtually erases or disregards everything on the outside of those boundary lines. Faulty framing then is defined by the mistaken and wrong setting and placements of boundaries for a viewpoint, topic or public argument and no matter whether on purpose or by design it erases or disregards far too much of the discourse information we as Crips need to properly resolve a matter. We are far too proud to be cut off and cut out so framing is dangerous.

e.g.#1. Disrespect is an automatic transgression that we won't tolerate however, everything done which we don't like or agree with must never just so quickly be framed as: "Disrespect" because then all the rest of the (cookie dough) information involved has been cut out and tossed aside. It becomes almost impossible to find resolve for such limited and highly toxic matters after they've been framed: disrespect.

The use of faulty framing with the Crip communities has become so common and volatile that it often occurs without us even being aware of any of it. We readily accuse folks of disrespect for anything from "Wreckless Eyeballing" (slave-jim-crow era terminology) simply looking at one of us or our females funny. Disrespect for triumphing over us in a particular sports game, dance/rap battle, car or cycle race or a head up fight. These are NOT to be framed as disrespect because our codes of death before dishonor kicks in then justifies our rage and whatever irrational reactions we unleash in response to being disrespected, this makes it faulty framing. Disrespect has to be held to a high standard so that when someone crosses such a line, then it can be what it is but no longer can we keep chopping each other down because of how something pissed us off and made us "feel"! Our lives, according to these holy Scriptures have to be more valuable than that! Real talk Crips!!!

We been losing our valuable lives on both sides of the blue steel gun blasts and assault rifles spitting flames because the dungeons and the graves keep swallowing us up whole like we're cotton candy, not really caring who was right or wrong. We bump into somebody at an overcrowded coachella function or in a dark club or house party and might spill our drink, if we immediately deem the civilian as one who is trying to disrespect us he ends up getting stomped out and left in a bad physical condition and we end up losing three good homies to serious time in the prison somewhere or youth authority all behind someone who was never disrespecting us from the jump. The way we frame stuff often pops into our own heads so this Script is putting us all on notice to slow down our faulty framework and to start thinking deeper from now on. Even seeking the fresh perspective of a fellow loved one. If two or more cousins can agree that "Disrespect" is the proper frame for something someone said or did then its proper but otherwise we can't be driven by or functioning off of our emotions cuz emotions aint Crip-like!

e.g. #2. Staying "DOWN", being "down" for this or that and just being recognized as a "down" ass homeboy or homegirl is another extremely common faulty frame which we must recognize, realize when its appropriate and ultimately refrain from overusing especially when its not appropriate. A frame totally shapes the entire conversation in a confined little circle where a true blue is almost forced to respond in the same soldier way. If one frames a task like running across a super highway as: "Are you Down?" its a faulty frame and a faulty premise because the downest Crip may not ever be down for running across a dangerous highway. The frame must be rejected otherwise a bred one can easily (as may often do) get drawn in to the premise of: "always be Down for yours?" as a well known and accepted Crip characteristic that must be exhibited, then be forced to uphold the high Crip integrity by doing whatever is framed, categorized or cast as being the "Down" thing to do. Faulty use of this frame has become so casual that the term of being "Down" has been diminished over the years and decades but its not dead. A Crip sticking to the Script is obviously as down as any human could be but younger, more twisted generations have on occasion cast "being down" as snitching or committing any number of transgressions against Crip law to save themselves or get revenge or whatever form of reasoning a twisted mind can conjure up to foul. Whereas when an unfortunate issue occurs in the ghetto where minorities have no one to empathize with their good intentions the frame the media will always cast the story in would be "Justice", thereby making the solution only be grounded in who did the right or wrong no more, no less! No compassion, no care! Other famous examples of faulty frame work of this nature can be found in the big landmark decision from the Roe v. Wade case. The rhetoric that the Nation still cant resolve despite the court's opinion is due in large part to how both are framed. One side's argument is framed in language which proclaims their position as "Pro-life" sounding obviously like such a simply decent and liberal disposition. This masterpiece of framework eliminates all the political jargon and asks you if you are for "Life" or you are not, its that simple. The frame lends itself to no other alternatives therefore no solutions are ever really, genuinely put on the table but these are Conservatives, Republicans and the like so in a pro-life context the liberals should all agree. Not so, cuz on the Democratic-Liberal side of the debate the framework is equally as masterful proclaiming the position of: "Pro-Choice" sounding obviously as simple and fair as we'd want our liberal party to sound. Who would dare deny our women their right to choose? No other facts or information is necessary to answer such a question. How something is framed often makes it impossible to see the opposing side of whatever the issue is. We as Crips have to start recognizing this bad tendency we have to frame something and then think with all our heart that we are righteous only because we've made it impossible to see the opposing side as clear as we should. In seconds a few words are exchanged and then comes the frame "You think I'm some punk bitch?" or... "You ain't nobody I gotta lie to" then whatever was the actual topic is eliminated from the frame so that all we see is this new picture that justifies straight violence. Any and every single dispute particularly between Crips who are sticking to the Script should and shall always re examine the frame because cousins working at the same objectives, who hold the same family values and who Love, for Life with Loyalty absolutely can not have long-lasting disputable facts between them, it's simply not possible. Even in regards to matters of the heart our strong Criplettes must stop abusing the frame of Love when they're upset: "You dont love me!" or... "If you really cared you'd do this or that!" Our females casting phrases like this cripples and immobilizes us intimately and our reactions often come out just as wreckless and irresponsibly depending on how disciplined or undisciplined a particular cousin might be. Our cousins female or male being too quick to frame petty disputes as: "They're jealous" or "haters" or "too stuck up on some OTHER shit!" etc... Frames of any sort are dangerous. These tactics and schemes are considered beautiful in the beholding eyes of lawyers, interpreters and arbiters who enjoy U.S. Constitutional Law because once you are a professional at casting and framing under the guaranteed protections of the law of the land then you can very handily decide what multi-billion dollar corporations deserve a compassionate break from paying taxes or who deserves Federal funds. Meanwhile the skilled legal counselors must also decide how to pitch Senate Bills and state codes that pits the minorities against themselves or the middle class against the minorities and poor to be criminalized and ultimately blamed for everyone's financial struggles. The examples of Constitutional frames which were craftily cast are too countless to demonstrate here but Here is where a Crip acquires the knowledge (like prescription glasses) to see it all for his and her self. We know the courage and honor our loved ones demonstrate out there in them hoods every single day with no pay, with no big media praise and no pension plans are exactly what U.S. soldiers do during their tours to military service in hostile lands except for one critical difference which is of course ... The Frame! Nonetheless, we can't Stop! Won't Stop! Refuse to be Stopped! Until the very last drip drops in the form of tears upon our Casket top!!!

Racism

Another of these commonly used and significantly abused faulty frames is that of "Racism" or the questioning of who we'll deem "The Racist". This frame originally when it was properly applied would always act as an alarm for both the accuser and the accused to check what they are doing and do better. This frame would invite the examining eyes of society's most decent folks who, following World War II became extremely indignant and eloquently opposed to any sorts of racism, Jewish, Black or other wise. America's criminal and moral indictment of Hitler and the Soviet Union was also a subsequent call for USA to deport herself as the Land of the free and the home of the brave (even morally) so that during the civil rights era, being called a "Racist" or actually exhibiting "Racism" resembled that deplorable criminal and moral indictment we'd associated Hitler with. Americans, although so many were spitting, kicking, yelling and hating Blacks, the comparison of this great Nation to that deplorable Soviet Union was far too much to consider. So, even after American racist began bombing churches and slaughtering women and children, the American Associated Press showed a patriotic duty as well as a fiduciary responsibility to at least minimize the damage to the strong and positive image America would maintain. The accusations of "Racism" and/or what we deem as "Racist" acts by a government, a corporation, a public service or a private industry suddenly had a high threshold to meet unless it was flat out admitted. The accusers were shamed into believing or at least considering the possibility that they were "over reacting" (even by other Blacks who held prominent or influential positions) and they themselves even getting cast as "playing the victim" or "playing the race card!" which no respectable person ever wanted to be seen as doing. Finally this became the long standing and ever-so-effective "faulty frame".

Here are some notable examples of faulty frameworks which were promoted by the Associated Press and that totally galvanized the well-intentioned whites along with the socialites of color towards embracing racisms of all kinds (even some genocidal designs) all in the name of doing the right thing: #1. The War on Crime. (Blacks, Whites and Puerto Ricans were often jailed-criminalized-for peaceful public protestings).

#2. The War on Gangs/Communist Radicals (People of Color were often considered as unreasonable radicals, commie-sympathizers and co-operatives, hate speakers and gang members) all of which who needed to be jailed in order for America to continue to prosper. #3. The War on Poverty. (Welfare and Social Security checks, government housings and county hospitals all contingent on folks docile compliance e.g. women with children, (young girls) must break up with the child's father to qualify for the money and housing, thus forever fracturing the family dynamic for most.) #4. The War on Drugs. (Sophisticated drugs and foreign guns mysteriously appear in abundance beyond what anyone could imagine rendering everyone at higher risk of dying, being addicted to drugs, dealing drugs and absolutely ending up dead or in jail.) #5. The War on Education which is cleverly disguised as: Prison expansions equals more new jobs and redistricting political capital, i.e. rural area's gain power. #6. The sinister frame work around racism now makes it nearly impossible to ever be adequately identified and addressed for society's moral benefit however for the C-Nation there are a few civilian notables they've missed:

A.) The 1st black president is initially loved and celebrated by the entire world so racism attacked and cast what was unprecedented world unity (rallied under U.S.A.) into several faulty frames such as "they think Obama is Jesus!", "he's a celebrity President with no record of leadership", "the Media is drinking the Kool-Aid", its just "White guilt!" and "being critical of the presidency isn't racist, its patriotic!" until finally the great pivot occurs so that other Nations are now uncooperative and hostile.

B.) The American Supreme Court justices finally articulate "cause" to overturn landmark (1965) voter's rights legislation that was put in place to combat racisms throughout the USA.

C.) Major magazines and media personalities all sway the Nation to accept a millionaire's ridiculous explanation for referring to blacks using "Niggers!", Several of the docile Socialites immediately jump on board. A national broadcasting network eagerly vindicates her.

D.) Affirmative action is sent back to State Courts assuring eventually it will also die.

E.) A grown man guns down a black child in a hoodie and is admired during trial.

F.) The greatest humanitarian and entertainer is (in death) continuously ridiculed as a pedophile through most of the major T.V. networks (albeit inadvertedly) even until one of his three small children attempts suicide, then the media blames the family for this. The faulty framework that protects, conceals and/or qualifies racism here in America is so subtle and widely practiced that even the victims of racism find it difficult to righteously explain-prove-prosecute in this type of stupefied court of public opinion. There will always be apologetic racist, there will always be the argument of a racist who had been around, employed or even befriended several blacks in the course of their lives. Therefore the faulty frame that obscures the true picture from honest eyes simply must be removed. No more qualifying these offenses and slurs by comparing whether or not the accused racist has ever done good or tries to say it was a mistake. Hell yea, being racist is a mistake but moreso its a character flaw which melanin deficient human must purposely fight off and for this reason, a charge of racism should and shall only be disproved in our eyes -via- that person, that government branch or agency, that public service, that corporation, or private industry, etc... that people's body of work leading up to that accusation is to stand alone as a representation of what he/she or they are genuinely all about. i.e. They've been actively contributing to non-racist solutions. They make routine gestures that employ and/or educate folks of color. He/she or they have a track record of deliberate investments in a specific black family's goal or dream. etc...

America is a racist Nation to its core and this is true even to this day because of the many faulty frames that stay in place to define for us (in a faulty way) what racism actually is. For example: During hurricane Katrina, once the levy fell the wards that make up the ghetto inner city of New Orleans were flooded. The media and the justice system quietly exonerated the local whites who shot and killed all the black men, women and children who tried to seek refuge in their community. The faulty frame simplified their racist behavior as: "Good folks in fear were only trying to protect their families and their town from all the looters and the violence". The true frame of this picture should have empathized with the victims by suggesting: "Those were good folks in flight for their lives from a disaster like none of them had ever seen before. They merely wanted to live!". Racism is most visible once you learn the trickery and power of the framework, the context and how a story is cast. As Crips who stick to these holy Scriptures... Real Eyes "Realize" Real Lies!!!

Manhood

Another faulty frame which is commonly used by some homegirls is: manhood. There are arguments and accusations which tend to get heated but never is it justified when we decide to frame the discourse in the perimeter of manhood by implying that: "A Real Man" would do this or he wouldn't have done that. This is a faulty frame which when used only manipulates and/or disqualifies the entire talking process. Being a man is a biochemical actuality of ones "Y" chromosomes to his "X" chromosomes in which the male typically has two unlike sex chromosomes and the female's "X" chromosomes are usually paired. This is what determines man from woman, male from female. Manhood is not something that can be morally or ethically earned, secured or forfeited. The faulty premise of stepping up to be a: "Real Man" only survived through the racial era and was resurrected for the young generations through talk shows and media mainly to be a tool of self-destruction.

Any manchild, any young man and any elder man from any particular one of the Crip Cadres all hold masculinity as a quintessential element in their manhood or mischaracterizing or engaging in faulty framing becomes a very dangerous, highly toxic approach to any male Crip and can often spark an unexpected and exaggerated response.

Recognizing faulty framework when its being cast by media, by politicians, movies and/or television shows in critical for the community at large because in the function of capitalism (economic domination) and imperialism (social domination) the definitions of who is the "real men" and who are the righteous and "trustworthy men" hold all of the importance. Once women turn on/against manhood they become no more than docile concubines and reproduction machines with an income and reliable impulse or predisposition for spending/buying back into a system that destroyed their men.

Common criticisms against our high profile athletes, entertainers and actors in similar fashion all agree that a "real man" would never hit a woman. Although we as Crips don't advocate men hitting women, it is an unfortunate reality that does occur within some relationships and/ or during their turbulent times, nonetheless, their issue is the action of him hitting her and not that he is not a man. The society that despises them both tends to cast their unfortunate feuding in the most damaging & deceptive framework possible thereby derailing their love entirely. Attacking a male Crip is a faulty frame for this obvious reason which is: There can be no reasoning or reconciliation where a Crip is forced to defend his manhood. So, unlike the civilian society that is fine with seeing both the man and woman walk away alone, we cast these contentious and violent relationships in the proper frame, calling them "Toxic"! This then avoids putting the man on the defense and the woman on the offense but places them both at the face of their relationship itself and more realistically positioned to resolve, to separate or reconcile without the weaponized criticisms trying to dictate the outcome.

"Being a Man!" is also commonly cast to frame ones deplorable decisions such as: (1) Rebelling, (2) Absconding or, (3) Snitching. e.g. Rebelling is when one or more resists or revolts against authority which in our case would be our Crip government, the holy Faculty. For an argument can be made on behalf of manhood (being a Man) that doesn't need and won't tolerate a circle of people making decisions about how one lives his life. Secondly Absconding is when one or more decides to secretly depart or hide from the cadre-family as that argument could easily be framed as: it took a "real man" to walk away and be his own man! Finally, the Snitching framework which explains that, in order to tell the truth you must first just: "Man-up!" to the situation, stop thinking like some one's little soldier boy & "Although its hard to snitch, "Being a man" means doing whats right!" etc...

Faulty Framing exists all through out the common dialogue, the cliches and childhood fairy tales so that whenever the right strings are manipulated, ones mind begins to recall the moral lessons imbedded within us, then we yield to implied "right things to do" all the time.

Within this huge Crip world of ours, the male cousin has aesthetic masculine traits which should not be discouraged, distrusted or denied and our women-folk shall not be the victims of our manhood but the direct recipient of it and all its benefits and wonders because they complete us in the Yin-Yang dynamic and together we are absolutely the C.R.I.P.S the Community Raised Infantry Progressing. Loved by few, hated by many, respected by All!!!

VI. Incarcerations Nation

Out of the night that covers me, Black as a pit from pole to pole

I thank whatever gods may be, for my uncomparable soul

At the thrill of clutch and circumstance I have not winced or cried aloud

Under the bludgeoning of hate my head is bloodied but unbound

Beyond this place of wrath and tears looms the horrors of the shade

And yet the menace of the years birds and shall bind me unafraid

It matters not how straight the gate or how charred with punishment is the scroll

I am the Master of my fate, I am the Captain of my Soul

- Invictus
(Nelson "Madiva" Mandela 28 yrs.)

Penological Pomp And Circumstance

Every since the dawn of civilization, every since the agricultural revolution proposed to and then married Imperialism, every since the two became One, everything has changed (especially in America.) They conceived a love child who'd reign supreme, a love child who'd remain a permanent fixture in our society, a notorious love child whose first, middle and last name is familiar to everyone yet only those of "us" worthy of this Holy Script shall know his full name intimately. Sir Justice Torturous Incarceration. It is by this name that three horrific eras of government dictatorship comes into clear view for us to see. Sir Justice started under only this first name and as an infant child was weaponized by Pharaohs, Kings, Queens, Popes and Soldiers to shape and bend each society to their will, even among others they nailed Jesus Christ to a cross in the name of Justice. Then, centuries later, as Justice reached his terrible teens he became callous and methodically cruel thereby earning his middle name: "Torturous" marking the era to be known as the "Medieval" or Middle ages, with newly heinous (yet entertaining) distributions of justice that far exceeded Augustus, Julius or Pontius' furnaces and coliseums where folks were simply burned or eaten alive. Sir Justice Torturous was now in his prime and had the greatest expert/scientific minds at work designing the most diabolical contraptions known to mankind (e.g. iron maiden, guillotines, wheels, etc...) most of which are too sick and sinister to pronounce even... however, throughout this purely gruesome period the Machiavellian doctrine coaxed him to evolve and mature out of the dark ages of crusades, famines, witch hunts, black plagues, wars, massacres, Inquisitions and such, in order to explore adulthood now...thoroughly! And with adulthood the young Sir Justice Torturous would become less temperamental and have to master the arts of deception along with the techniques of demonization. These are the priceless pearls that effectively articulated the philosophy of "Divine Right" and thereby did deliver to him the riches of all the other Continents and Islands on the planet even by invading them, conquering them and enslaving the native inhabitants of them with impunity. It is at this juncture that Sir Justice Torturous would finally secure his last name, a name that's Constitutionally and Democratically protected even until this day after slavery was outlawed. A name that everyone recognizes and romanticizes as our necessary evil, the name that ties in perfectly with the first and second names beautifully... Incarceration!

The effectiveness and precision of these new techniques (verbal slanderings and demonizations) worked remarkably well in Europe and the Americas but became a bit more visible around 1846 when the U.S.

declared war on Mexico then took California and the State of New Mexico then add in the 1861 Civil War mentality with the huge influx of immigrants after that great potatoe famine in Ireland as seen in the movie "Gangs of New York" the rhetoric was getting real nasty. Then in 1898-99 America quietly supported revolts world wide but especially in Cuba which would become the playground for the American Mobsters-Politicians and Entertainers after World War I ended (1914-1918). By 1918 America was quick to pass a new "Alien Act" (or Alien and Sedition Act) designed to: "exclude and expel from the United States aliens who are members of the anarchist classes." This vague and ambiguous type of language makes for a perfect weapon against whomever you choose as long as you dress them up as an anarchist. Suddenly but surely now down comes the rains... Hatemongers were taking center stage behind their divisive words, positioning themselves for legitimacy: German economy collapses (aprx. 1927), while all of Europe suffers a man whom (A. Hitler) emerges and blames the Jews seeking legitimacy to cleanse and restructure the world; Mussolini rants and bangs his way throughout Rome, Italy (1922); J. Edgar Hoover accrues an annual budget of 2.25 million and an almost 700 man staff to persue "political undesirables" conducts "Red raids" and to flourish from the so called "slacker raids" of 1918 aimed at all young men who hadn't enlisted for war to the so called "Gang busters" and "war on crime" where Congress authorized this fairly new Bureau to collect (then file in data bases) the finger prints of even law abiding citizens in 1930. Legitimacy was coming forward boldly as government propaganda (congregatio de propaganda fide ~ Congregation for propagating the faith; organization established by Pope Gregory XV to spread information) both in the Old world as well as in the New World. Jews (and gypsies) were blamed for alot of the economic woes of Europe and were relegated to segregated areas and oddly enough the Jews area was called: "Ghettos". Their segregation was fine with them and economically they thrived from supporting each other's own businesses and social lifestyles until they were ultimately rounded up, their wealth was confiscated and they were "incarcerated", used for labor then slaughtered. The Expropriations and genocide visited on the Jews in their ghettos largely contributed to their empathy and bonds with the blacks in America as the hate wore its way into the very fabric of the new world in much of the same fashions.

Harlem's
Realest

The 1915 movie: "Birth of a Nation" was the propaganda legitimizing hate from all whites towards criminalized blacks according to the Klans. Then from 1917-1921 race riots across all of America as whites marched into "Ghettos" to loot, burn and kill everything relative to blacks. One particular example unfolded in Tulsa, Oklahoma which between 1921-23 was known as the "Magic City" probably because of the nearby Glen Pool oil fields, the heavily populated (segregated) black area which became the first black Wallstreet or perhaps because of the Nations #2 largest Klan that fiercely enforced the segregation. In 1921 while the black dollar circulated around the booming black business area at the streets of: Greenwood, Archer and Pine (one of many music groups emerged and the most famous of them was the "G.A.P. band" which is named after these streets) Economic woes angered the local Klan of about 3,200 members not counting the very 1st Jr. Klan of boys 12 yrs-18 yrs old or the Nation's largest "all women" sect. who suddenly decided to seek out and murder 19 yr. old Dick Rowlands-via-castration for alleged "improper" conduct toward a white girl. Normally the blacks would have ignored it but the Klans yearly quota had already been satisfied, they'd already lynched 64 boys and men, 4 were burned up, 17 were shot and two were drowned so this time the black Tulsans said "No!". Several WWI veterans poured out of the black choc-shops (adult bars) and stores to shield the young boy from the violent mob outside the Courthouse-Police Station on the white side of the street. The astonished-hooded whites began ransacking the black side of town then left and returned in deputized uniforms to arrest and "Incarcerate" aprx. 4,000 black men, women and children under declarations of Marshall law. The Red Cross and Military Commission arranged for mostly everyone to be released with the orders to clean the ash and rubble of over 1,115 burned homes plus aprx. 314 looted but unburned hotels, stores and other homes and businesses in the black area only to be told to collect free bus tickets "to leave" their business and homes behind. Ironically when ever a mass movement stick up like this is done by white folks in the name of White Supremacy its called: "Expropriations" and no one knows this better than the Jewish who as a people would experience it some 16 yrs. later against almost 7 times as many home owners, business owners and families on a night forever known as Kristallnacht (night of broken glass), November 9th, 1938 except instead of the free bus ticket out, which the Red Cross provided here in America to us, an aprx. 26,000 Jewish men, women and children from Germany to Austria were marched into (Incarceration) concentration camps in the name of justice. It is quieted, concrete truths like this that male kinships between Blacks and Jews. We've worked together, marched together, suffered together, loved together and prospered together and Supremacist are well aware that they could never take the Jews again without first defeating us, the blacks in America and Europe, The Crips... We call this unwritten contract "Ghetto Love!". They set off the first official: "Ghetto - Uprisings" in January and April of 1943 in Warsaw to protest all the "final solution" round-ups and killings (in true genocidal fashion) yet by "May" the entire Warsaw ghetto had been exterminated. Now as we find ourselves relegated into our own local ghettos being rounded up and/or killed by cops (in the genocidal fashion) the true among us recognize history respectfully and acknowledge Jewish people as our ghetto cousins of the struggle.

Incarcerations have become an accepted house guest and respected pillar in all of American society however, Sir Justice Torturous Incarceration hasn't been faithful in his marriage to Mrs. Agriculture and in fact we've learned that he has had this mistress for a long, long time and her name is Ms. Industrial revolution. This lady is all about money and how best to capitalize off of anyone and anything absolutely! So then, after all of this Pomp and Circumstances which we've learned to live with, now we know the circumstances were a facade and perhaps pharisaically administered on certain people and/or against certain communities arbitrarily especially ever since Incarcerations and warehousing folks for Life became so profitable. What could anyone have expected when (during the height of all these Black and Jewish uprisings against White Supremacy) a bunch of known White Supremist are given Millions of dollars, Absolute National power (as the Federal Bureau of Investigations) & whose livelihood and job security is contingent on the existence of crime and is led by one J. Edgar Hoover who personally despised blacks and considered their Jewish sponsors as subversives or anarchist whom under his recently passed Espionage Act and/or the Alien and Sedition Act (passed 1918 to "exclude and expel from the U.S.A. aliens who are members of the anarchist classes") could be targeted themselves for deportations or black listed (at the least) which usually caused social and economic disaster. America's Justice system was basically designed, constructed and erected primarily from racist stock, even as if World War One left the Nation thirsty for human blood. The Justice department (Sir Justice Torturous Incarceration) fell into league with one of the most racist vigilante organizations, the A.P.L. (American Protective League) recruiting over 250,000 so-called "loyal citizens" across the country who could (without training) go buy a badge for one dollar and virtually become the law under the title: "Auxiliary to the U.S. Department of Justice". Its painfully obvious that the Pomp and Circumstance type of language which pitted one race against the others (as their superior) did find its welcomed refuge within (and under) the color of law. It is with knowledge such as this that we actually feel the social atmosphere that ruled those days, weeks, months and years that followed shortly there after. The slaughterings of black communities from Rosewood, Florida to Tulsa, Oklahoma and so many, many more. Maybe inspiring the Whites (Supremacist) throughout Europe that led to the legalized annihilations of all non whites (aprx. 6 million Jews and 9 million Gypsies, Slavs, Poles, Ukrainians, Belarussians, homesexuals and disabled as well) all exterminated in pursuit of a pure White Supreme race in police state fashion. Such Pomp and such circumstances as had never been heard or seen before. Suddenly, upon the advent of World War II a great concession (or perhaps it should be called a reconciliation) occurred in the U.S.A. so that everyone who "looked" White in any of its generic forms was now accepted so long as they exhibit an almost rabid patriotism so that when President Roosevelt ordered all Japanese and Japanese Americans had to be rounded up and Incarcerated (February, 1942-1945) it basically went through without a hitch. Yes, Incarceration has been and will remain to be the fruit that White Supremacy bares, however White Supremacy does not always manifest through hate or aggressive racisms especially once it drains through the filter of education. Modern day White Supremacy is intelligently shrouded below seemingly righteous desires to create a better society and world, today the method is more subtle and much easier to be universally qualified by the media so we are duty-bound to get laced by sticking to the Script so that we can better recognize and deal with this monster successfully.

After President Roosevelt's Order regarding the Japanese Incarcerations ran their course President Harry S. Truman's term came and on March

22nd 1947 his E.O. (Executive Order) #9835 required the Justice dept. (Sir Justice Torturous Incarceration) to draw up a list of organizations to be considered "totalitarian, fascist, communist or subversive... or seeking to alter the government of the U.S. by unconstitutional means". By 1954 the F.B.I. had placed hundreds of groups - including the Chopin Culture Center, the Cervantes Fraternal Society, the Committee for Negro Arts, the Committee for the Protection of the Bill of Rights, the League of American Writers, the Nature Friends of America, the Washington Bookshop Association, and the Yugoslav Seamen's Club-on the proscription list, all compliments of that "Truman Doctrine" proclamation-.(see "Agents of Repression" By. Ward Churchill & Jim VanderWall).

Meanwhile, countless tiny pockets of black resistance rose up and fell down throughout the Nation as the various prominent black civil rights leaders would show up to address local police and Klansmen forces by teaching the local blacks first & foremost to become apathetic to Incarcerations. (Martin Luther King Jr, Malcolm-X, Huey P. Newton, Eldridge Cleaver, Stokely Carmichael, Assata Shakur, H. Rap Brown, Bunchy Carter. George and Jonathan with Angela Davis, Elaine Brown, etc...) going to jail was par for the course.

"The Cointelpro operations of the 1960s were modeled on the successful programs of earlier years undertaken (by the Government) to disrupt the American communist party...[which] continued through the 1960's with such interesting variations as Operation Hoodwink from 1966-1968, designed to incite organized crime against the Communist Party through documents fabricated by F.B.I. evidently in the hope that criminal elements would carry on the work of repression and disruption in their own manner, by means that may be left to the imagination."

- Noam Chomsky, COINTELPRO.

The infamous "operation Hoodwink" particularly targeted the various hoods in the black ghettos where "street knowledge" and "codes for Criminal Conduct" was all the people knew and although the government by this time had thoroughly put in check almost every race (Blacks, Jewish, Irish, Italian, Japanese, Koreans, Natives, Mexicans, Cubans, Jamaicans, Russians, Puerto Ricans and Haitians, etc...) still no one knew they'd stoop to these new lows which they mastered in the name of Counter Intelligence

Programs which (as renowned Historian Mr. Chomsky explained briefly) did trick us, manipulate us, weaponized and ultimately hood winked us (street gangs) to attack civil rights and grass roots parties as rival gangs and they became equally hostile towards us and each other just as was insidiously planned by the Bureau.

While in strict F.B.I. parlance a Cointelpro refers to a specific secret and typically illegal operation (there were many thousands of individual COINTELPROs executed between 1940-1971), in popular usage the term came to signify the whole context of clandestined political repression activities, (initially targeting the Socialist Workers Party and Communists 1940's-50's and manipulating the Mobs to war with the Unions in the Prohibition era) yet regardless of its precise technical meaning in "Bureauese", COINTELPRO is now used as a descriptor covering the whole series of sustained and systemic campaigns directed by the Bureau against a wide array of selected domestic political organizations and individuals especially during the 1960s (there were more than 2,370 separate "literary" COINTELPROs - Internal Security - RACIAL MATTERS) even as Black revolutionaries were radicalizing all other non-whites under their over simplified color schemes (Red, yellow, brown) to rise up and organize, the Bureau in colaboration with local police units functioned in varying degrees of intensity to disrupt all forms of unity, progress movements and solidarity teachings that sprouted from these grassroots minority goups. These were the methods Cointel Pro's effectively mastered:

1. Eavesdropping - A massive surveillance program predicated on intelligence gathering but in actuality a group called C.C. (Citizens Commission) broke into F.B.I. headquarters of Media in Pennsylvania on March 8th, 1971 and retrieved documents using the word "Paranoia" as its political repression vernacular, to be induced among the targeted groups-via-wire taps surreptitious entries, burglaries, mail tamperings, electronic devices, live "tails" and so on.

2. Bogus Mail - Fabrications of correspondences between members was the designs that fostered "splits" between high ranking friends and other organizations. Their success is most notable for the split between (friends and Black Panther Party leaders)

Huey B. Newton and Eldridge Cleaver per FBI memo dated: 12-3-1970 - L.A. field office (page 2) it recommends a letter be forged and sent ostensibly by a disgruntled Party member: "... provoke Cleaver to openly question Newton's leadership... It is felt that distance and lack of personal contact between Newton and Cleaver do offer a counterintelligence opportunity that should be probed... [Additionally] each division [of the F.B.I.] should write numerous letters [under similar circumstances] to Cleaver criticizing Newton's leadership. It is felt that, if Cleaver received a sufficient number of complaints regarding Newton it might... create dissension that later could be more fully exploited."

3. "Black Propaganda" Operations - The mass distributions of fabricated publications (leaflets, broadsides, etc...) "on behalf of" targeted organizations and/or individuals which misrepresents their positions, goals or objectives in such a way to foster discredits & tensions. Notably the FBI's J. Edgar Hoover explained in a Memo dated: Nov. 25, 1968 "recipient offices are instructed to submit imaginative and hard-hitting counter-intelligence measures aimed at crippling the B.P.P." -via- "gang warfare". They published cartoon caricatures both of violence between Ron Karenga's - United Slaves" versus Black Panthers in Los Angeles and ultimately caused the United States org. to shoot L.A.'s Panther Leaders Jon Huggins and our Alprentice "Bunchy" Carter Jan. 17th 1969 in UCLA's Campbell Hall and this angered and inspired the formation of the L.A. Crips.

4. Disinformation or "Gray Propaganda" - The F.B.I. would release disinformation to the press to foster more tensions and to discredit voices of reason or peace proposals.

5. Harassment Arrests - The repeat arrests of targeted individuals creating paranoia, depleting funds for bail bonds, and of course generating mass convictions/Incarcerations.

6. Infiltrators and Agents Provocateurs - The placement of agents into legitimate groups only to engage in illegal activities (and or rebelliousness from within) to destroy progress. Both these tactics of harassments and infiltrations were aggressively used against B.P.P.'s Maxwell Sanford who founded the New York

chapter in Aug. 1966 then his own R.A.M. (Revolutionary Action Movement) which was heavily targeted in Philadelphia by 1967. This same year that Black and White interracial marriages was begrudgingly legalized.

7. Pseudo - Gangs - FBI provocateurs (notably Joe Burton between 1972-75) created organizations all over the U.S.A. to unify with legitimate grassroots movements and to war with others. One notable group in Tampa, Florida called: "Red Star Cadre" who hated the Crips.

8. Bad Jacketing - Snitch jacketing or bad jacketing refers to the practice of creating distrust and suspicions where there should be none. F.B.I. documents claims this tactic did "isolate and eliminate" organizational leaders. Most notable is the Cointelpro's submission dated July 10th 1968 where rumors were manufactured against one Stokely Carmichael the leader of SNCC (Student Non-violent Coordinating Committee) that he was a C.I.A. informant, this proposal by the SAC (Special Agent in Charge) reads:

... One method of accomplishing [this] would be to have a carbon copy of an informant report reportedly written by Carmichael to C.I.A. carefully deposited in the automobile of a close friend to promote distrust between Carmichael and the Black Nationalist community. It is also suggested that we inform a certain percentage of reliable criminals and racial informants "We heard Carmichael is a CIA informant".

(Another proposal which was approved in the same sinister spirit directed at Carmichael): "On 7/4/68, a pretext phone call was placed to the residence of Stokely Carmichael and his mother is told it was a friend of Carmichael's fearful of the future safety of her son. It was explained to Mrs. Carmichael the absolute necessity for Stokely to 'hide out' was much as several BPP members were out to kill him sometime this week. Mrs. Carmichael appeared shattered/shocked and stated she would tell Stokely when he came home."

On September 5th, 1970 Huey P. Newton-B.P.P. minister

of defense release a statement that: "We... charge that Stokely Carmichael is operating as an agent of the CIA"

These Counter Intelligence Programs proved even more effective to and among Prisoners inside.

9. Fabrication of Evidence - A widely used FBI tactic used against key individuals whom refuse to snitch or lie for agents against comrads. The fabrication of hard evidence, the withholding of exculpatory evidence, the intimidations of witnesses and coercions of false testimony, fake letters threatening the jury in the panther's Chicago 8 trial, or the Panther 21 in New York all the way to the present day as numerous deathrow cases fall apart. Incarcerations was and is the fate that awaits many of the most true. All of these well documented counterintelligence programs are sinister yet sophisticated by design toward the same end, Incarcerations and/ or death.

10. Assassinations and Expansions of Cointelpro Operations - Assassination programs are the most sinister of all and although they are the most difficult to prove, an eery sense of "knowing" plagues the entire nation. From the Hoffa and Mafia disappearances, to the civil rights leaders (M.L. King Jr.) to President Kennedy and many others, the entire world over, kills did expand.

The instituting and the Nation's docile acceptance of all these COINTELPRO's is the perfected display of Penological Pomp and Circumstance anyone had ever seen or heard of before. Even targeting our other cousins of the struggle, the Puerto-Ricans, the Bureau's leader Hoover himself stated:

"The Bureau is considering the feasibility of instituting a program of disruption to be directed against organizations which seek independence for Puerto Rico... In considering this matter you should bear in mind that the Bureau desires to disrupt the activities of these organizations and is not interested in mere harassment" - August 4th, 1960

So then, as this humongous Crip National of ours evolves out of the criminal crash dummy box we once proudly lived in, we won't slip on these tactical banana peels the way we did long ago. Our focus is like a laser, our minds are of steel and our hearts are of stone therefore a Commitment to Excellence becomes our new Modus Operandi so, from city to city, state to state, Island to Island & Country to Country we shall consolidate with legal endeavors in all different languages and cultures for prosperity in Love, Life and Loyalty. Death before Dishonor is the only reason why they kill us or call us crazy but in truth we're now spitting out these Crip Scriptures becuz History told us to...

"Throughout history, it has been the inaction of those who could have acted, The indifference of those who should have known better, and the silence of those voices of justice when it mattered most that made it possible for evil to triumph..."

- Haile Selassie
(Emperor of Ethiopia).

"Death fades into insignificance when compared to a life of imprisonment. To spend each night in jail, day after day, year after year gazing at the bars and longing for freedom is indeed expiation..."

- Lewis E. Lawes, Warden
Sing Sing Prison, 1920-41.

Incarceration Nation
Conquering Confinements

"Grasping the reality of our Crip situation, it becomes essential to us that we learn to Overstand and conquer the ever so destructive traits of confinement that plague us generation after generation. The immediate effects and the residual effects of confinements visited upon us in various ways have been annihilating to us and for our families for far too long and so finally we have evolved..."

- Almasi Kamau Shakur

And the Lord God said, "It is NOT GOOD that man should be alone; I will make him a helper comparable to him."

- Genesis 2:18

In this Consolidated Crip Nation of ours there is the dynamic of family at its core. This dynamic exists in every single tribe, hood, clique, island, team and cadre. The fathers, Uncles, Mothers, Aunts, brothers, sisters, cousins and kids.

An incarceration of one is an incarceration of that whole family therefore we shall herein learn to conquer the cruel and deliberate effects such incarceration wrecks on us. We each are duty-bound according to our Love, our Life and our Loyalty to fulfill our particular role and to usher each other through this demoralizing scheme and here are some of the basic characteristics and cures we must each stay mindful of.

First, anxiety, frustration and fear sets in often immediately upon the arrest. We're anxious and full of adrenaline at the thought that we are in the hands of our enemy who certainly mean us no good, this ignites the frustration and the fear. This first stage is potentially dangerous for some as the adrenaline surge tends to make some folks feel desperate to talk to someone, to know what their fate is, to negotiate the terms of their surrender and ransom. Most K-9s, detectives and agents are also taught about this first stage so that they can possibly magnify it and exploit it, however, as true Crips we are to maintain our composure, inhale and exhale and contact your cadre's C-Team. Every Crip family must protect its body and soul by having a home and phone number specifically set up to accommodate loved ones facing confinement so that no folks of ours ever have to feel so desperate and alone.

As stated above, a true Crip will maintain his or her composure and endure this first stage and move quickly into the second stage which usually consists of certain feelings of regret, guilt and a sense of urgency about the loose ends that need to be tied up. The C-Team members are committed to excellence and the execution of whatever unexecuted deeds a loved one has left behind if they can. It is absolutely critical to a confined person's stability that he/she never feels a bit of abandonment or disregard because Incarceration tends to make even the strongest loved one experience some level of insecurity. Depending on the circumstances and the magnitude of the case, the charges and the evidence, this second stage could involve some feelings of betrayal, bitterness and deep depression for certain homies or homegirls that aren't mentally and emotionally equipped to handle hearing things like "Capital Punishment" or "Life in prison" so they must be especially catered to and if some sort of betrayal did land him or her in such a situation, they shall be assured that the cadre will rectify the situation in an excellent form and fashion. It is us who invented the term: "God forgives... The Crips don't!!!" and we mean it.

This second stage involves such a wide range of emotional challenges for one on the inside whether he or she is confined in juvenile hall, camp or youth authority or whether he or she is in a county jail, a state prison or a federal penitentry, our cadre has the absolute duty and obligation to be on point and functioning at their full potential to head off all these typical emotions a loved one will be feeling so that they never reach stage three.

This third stage is the most dangerous and deplorable stage a person in confinement can sink to. The criminal minds experts call this their "break through" moment yet in truth any decent human being would clearly see this as an emotional "break down" moment. In the third stage one of the most dangerous characteristics a person begins to exhibit is his or her own egomania. Incarcerations without the proper balance of C-team love and an overstanding of the circumstances of legacy, a person slips into whats called "Me" mode. An ego gets so inflated that it opts to destroy everything within its reach all in the name of self preservation. Detectives first sobering attack will aim at a person's sense of "self".

Interrogators immediately want to establish to whomever they are targeting that "Your homies left you for dead!" or "The plea bargain goes to which ever one of you is smart enough to save your 'self'!" or "What kinda' man would put a woman he claims to love in such a position as this guy just put 'YOU' in?" etc... The tactics are countless and constantly evolving so any cadre sticking to the Script shall have a functioning faculty and therein a C-Team specifically assembled to keep and protect its hood's incarcerated body and soul intact. This third stage ego mania also manifests its "Self" -via- an incarcerated loved one's exaggerated self importance, with very little compassion or regard for anyone else. For example: Abusing the Cadre's resources or monopolizing their sponsor's time, instigating wars or undue violence merely because he or she can and/or indulging in any risky behavior that puts the whole hood family at risk unnecessarily.

This third stage, much like the second and first all stem from the emotions that an incarcerated loved one may experience to various degrees. Being incarcerated will enhance a Crips lusts and desires and from lusts and desires unquenched comes the inevitable feelings of disappointment. Masturbation should be controlled and done in some degree of moderation otherwise it absolutely will consume any individual's body and soul subsequently making him or her an overly emotional and flawed loved one. Intimacy is a dessert to be enjoyed only periodically not excessively by a strong soldier because it balances all that is cold and hard in us so that we are capable of feeling soft and warm. It is for this reason that even our loved ones on the outside find themselves having more emotions than they actually can use. (e.g. Anger is merely the emotionalized response to feelings of hurt or vulnerability). We should grow to master our lusts and desires knowing that the mastering of these vices produces a sort of Crip god or goddess.

"Where is the source of human grief, lamentation, pain and agony? Is it not to be found in the fact that people are generally desirous... clinging obstinately to lives of pleasure, excitement, self indulgence, ignorant of the fact that the desire for these very things is the source of human suffering." - The Teachings of Buddha (causations)

So then, as is our sworn duty, we as the C-family shall protect ours from these three stages of emotions regarding Incarcerations knowing that these are the times that truly tests and try a man's soul... So say the C-Team, our Body and Soul team.

Likewise there are all sorts of emotional tests and trials that attack our loved ones on the outside and so it is also our sworn duty to exhibit Love, Life, and Loyalty by being considerate towards them and mindful that our Incarceration is also trying upon their souls as well and these are some of the notables.

Wives and live-in-girlfriends - The women who depend on us on a daily basis or whose daily program involves us in some way, they shall suffer immediately. e.g. If you were a source of transportation for her or the kids, a care giver, a source of income or even a physical provider of sex or protection.

The void you will leave within a female's life shall be devastating to her psyche (her soul) yet she knows the code we've consummated her into so she tries to adapt immediately, we should give her time. Our hood's C-Team house shall always be welcoming and franchise-able so that once the word is out that you're incarcerated she can either call and leave the kids there while she goes to work, she can allow the other homegirls in the same situation to move in and they all work together, or create carpooling routines that accommodate her until other vehicles are made available.

Our sons, brothers and young cousins will suffer the immediate shock of anxiety wondering how you might handle incarceration in all the dangers and challenges they themselves are cautioned might soon become their own fates. How you deport yourself under the pressure of incarceration shall live forever in their minds as either the standard or the soft and deplorable so be sure to guard your legacy. Stick to the scriptures at all costs and don't feed them from the emotional stages you've experienced. Don't transfer your regrets, your fears or doubts and dont instigate these emotions within them. e.g. You call from the County jail, you're aware that you are about to do a stretch of time away from your family, as the phone rotates to your boys, your young sons, brothers or cousins you feel you should lace them with the truth about what might be about to happen out there because you are sober, clear-minded and in one of the heightened state of mind emotional stages described herein so you warn them: "Y'all keep an eye out for yo' Momma just in case that fool Big Frank's ass start coming through there, ya' hear!?" or "Y'all stay away from the homies, don't trust them fools, they got me in here and now they're laughing!" - The variety of 1st and 2nd stage emotions you'll grapple with during the early stages of your incarceration are temporary but the greatest tragedy of being confined is the high possibility of making what is called a "Career decision". The temporary feelings you'll experience should not be released into the atmosphere to infect another because those young sons, brothers or cousins that rely on you will incorporate those feelings you feel and could be contracting an infectious deadly disease that transgresses the law of Love, Life and Loyalty from their first Love (which is YOU) and later on in life, might not even know why. Many homies have hidden feelings of insubordination which were communicated to them way back during their vulnerable child hood years, a virtual cancer just laying dormant until it can manifest and claim its carrying body's life. So then all three stages of subsequent emotions of incarceration are potential communicable diseases that one must retain responsibly until your C-Team can provide the medicine required. Our sons, young brothers and cousins need only to know that the C-Team can use their help and in the meantime you're still and always standing tall, through it all chanting Death before Dishonor. It is the projection of this attitude that our young locs must see (and absorb) to protect them in full... Mind, Body and Soul!

Our hood fathers, Elder brothers, Uncles and Sr. Cousins can, on the other hand, hear you vent some of your true frustrations and suspicions because they'll be objective and able to identify the early stages of Incarceration emotions from some of your genuine concerns and take the real issues to the Blue room for the Faculty to decide.

Our fathers, Elder brothers, Uncles and Sr. cousins usually have lost more than one Crip to the system and/or the same son more than once so the gravity of the whole situation for them is much more routine and flawless. Nonetheless we must remember to be considerate about how we utilize even them. Many older loved ones have had their own personal encounters with the trying times of incarceration and therefore might already be partial towards an abrupt reaction that mirrors the one they may have had when they were incarcerated. These incarceration issues are so real and absolutely are the real issues regarding a Crip's body and soul. Last but not least our dear Mothers, the mommas that raised us, Grandma's, stepmothers, Godmomma's, Hood momma's and our baby-mommas. Any and all mothers of an incarcerated Crip should and shall be cherished, admired and also considered under great pressure and stress upon learning about her loss (you) because this incarceration shall certainly be trying on her body and soul as well. All Crip Mothers, just like the Crip wives and live-in-girlfriends (previously mentioned) also may have a daily program that involved us even if it's something as simple as cutting the grass or helping her carry in her groceries or even attending church with her one Sunday, therefore this void in her life should not be overlooked at all. Our mothers should and shall be also given the C-Team contact information and in circumstances where a Crip or Criplette was her primary care-giver the C-Team shall franchise her home, move her into a home or arrange for that particular Crip's sponsor to move in with the mother and take over where ever he or she left off. It is essential to the morale of the entire cadre that our incarcerated homies mother's and even baby's mommas are cared for with excellence. Everyone is aware that they could very well be in the same position of being incarcerated and therefore they should and shall know that their dear mothers won't ever be left behind. As for baby's mommas and mothers who don't necessarily require the full weight of C-Team interventions they should and shall be afforded the opportunity to have the C-Team's contact information and an open-ended invitation to participate in the noble services of caring for their loved one's Body and Soul, i.e. helping out their community's C-Team for this is clearly a work that Scriptures mandated long ago.

"The Son of Man Will Judge the Nations"

v.31 "When the Son of Man comes in His glory and all the Angels with Him... All the Nations will be gathered before Him and He will separate them one from another...Then He will say to those... Depart from me you cursed into the everlasting fire...Then they will also answer Him saying, 'Lord when did we see You hungry, or thirsty, or a stranger, or naked or sick or IN PRISON and did not visit you. Then He will answer them saying 'Assuredly I say to you, inasmuch as you did not do it to one of the least of these, you did not do it to me. And these will go away into everlasting punishment but the righteous into eternal life." -Holy Bible, New King James Version. -Matthew 25:31-46

Protocols and Codes of Conduct

The protocols and codes of conduct for a cadré notorious for never giving a fuck, a cadre that is infamous for being "insane to the brain", this all seems to be a contradiction but thats only from the point of view of those on the outside looking in while from the inside we all know that there are rules and these rules if (or when) broken can very easily cost someone dearly.

First of all, upon your arrival into any sort of incarceration or confinement situation one should be prepared to show paperwork and/

or divulge the circumstances of your placement there. These types of verifications may vary for and throughout different States, Institutions and countries but the premise must remain because degenerate crimes, double agents and absconders have other dues to be paid. The premise is to know and confirm two things: 1.) Who is around you and 2) Where are you at? e.g. In California's adult facilities, one must be issued a 114-lock up order immediately upon being placed in any segregated housing (The hole) so the 114 is often referred to as one's Driver's license. In the juvenile facilities the information is usually given by word of mouth, nothing covert so if you're snitching or have done something foul, the staff are liable and wont even dare to put a child at risk and usually those types of children aren't foolish enough to try to blend in. Nonetheless, knowing your surroundings is a security issue never to be compromised! Also, e.g. 2). Where you're at can become extremely critical to your safety because if you're placed with P.C's on what California's system calls an S.N.Y. (Sensative Needs Yard) you'll notice that no one cares about your paper work or has no regard for the protocols and the general population will be made up of rapist, child molesters and fools who've killed their own parents, siblings or children, etc... and for a true to agree to exist among these shall him or herself become tainted and radio active in the eyes of the Cadre. So... Always know who is around you and also know for sure where you're at.

Once you've established the arrival protocols, the procedure itself puts all the comrads on notice and all the other codes of conduct will naturally kick in.

1) A new arrival, once cleared as righteous must be issued a care package that contains all the essentials (1-bar of soap, 1-Toothpase, 1-deoderant, 1-comb or brush if available, shower shoes, paper, minimum 3 stamped envelopes) and with the care package

KIWE KITTY PROTOCOL

1. One cell within each section should be designated as the holder / distributor of items in the Kiwe Kitty.
2. All comrades, when going to canteen, should (at the least) when spending $35.00 to $45.00 contribute $3.00 to the Kiwe Kitty. $1.00 for every $10.00 or 50 cents for every $5.00.

3. Any comrade who receives items from the Kitty should, if he is able, give back to the Kitty to ensure its abundance.

4. When comrades go to the canteen they should obtain a list from the designated cell regarding what may be needed to replace what has been given.

5. Comrades should inform the designated cell of whether or not he will make it to the canteen and what amount he will be able to contribute. It is up to the holder / distributor to determine whether or not anything is needed, or if the Kitty is full.

6. The holder / distributor of the Kiwe Kitty should mainly have a stockpile of the following items: toothpaste, soap, deodorant, paper, and envelopes. These are the necessities. Anything else a comrade contributes to the Kitty can be done so at his own discretion.

7. The holder / distributor should only provide one of each of these items, with the exception of a ½ deodorant, to each comrade upon his arrival.

8. Before any items are given, the holder / distributor of the Kitty should obtain a comrade's 114(d) lock-up order, 115, or any other karatazi kazi disclosing why he is amongst us. All other present comrades should let the arrivee know that this is an established protocol before any items are distributed.

9. If the arrivee does not have his karatazi and the holder of the Kitty deems him correct, or knows him, then it is to the holder's discretion to provide him with the necessities.

10. If the arrivee does have his karatazi, but refuses to allow the designated cell to review it, he gets NOTHING!

11. The holder / distributor should maintain a list of all that is in the Kitty to be made available to any comrade wishing to see it.

<u>ASANTE FOR YOUR COOPERATION</u>

The cadré receiving a new loved one should appropriately show the swagger that true Crips are known for by providing luxury items of its choice or befitting their particular circumstances. e.g. I've been greeted with everything from a T.V., Radio, bags of groceries, smokes and drinks or at other prisons where constant wars and lock downs have depleted the resources so much so that the care package is a half a bar of soap, a ⅓ stick of deodorant, a syrup packet worth of toothpaste and a super sharp knife with some state indigent stamped envelopes. The core characteristic of the protocol is the exercise of Love, Life and Loyalty even with some degree of transparency so that potential allies know to respect this new arrival and enemies know it'll cost if they disrespect this new arrival. All eyes are on certain codes of conduct as these as we can and will study their new arrivals to identify if/when bosses pull up. Additional codes of conduct are all circumstance based and shall only compliment the Blue-ish golden rule of Death Before Dishonor which rests at the core of all conduct.

1. Circumstances of war - we shall always be prepared and devise plans to win. We shall not be driven by emotions: (sadness, anger or fear). We shall defer to those of us whom are well-read students of warfare and not those particularly gifted in economic ventures or those involved in their personal, intimate affairs on the outside. We shall deport ourselves with dignity and always establish the highest levels of seriousness. e.g. A first Lieutenant, after a violent melee is found to have a stab wound to his torso, he refuses to be removed from the yard-via-a stretcher, he struggles to stand, push his chest out, his head up and at 6'5" he walks with dignity to get medical treatment. This is copied in similar fashion by football players who gives the audience a "thumbs up"! The morale of battle and between skirmishes is high effected by the conduct of a fallen soldier who indicates to those around him or her that: "I'm strong so fight on!"

2. Circumstances of Peace - We must use these seasons to re-stockpile, re-prepare, re-arrange and re-establish ourselves (-via-house cleaning) so that we remain strong and in accord for the next go' round. We shall exhibit no residual signs of emotions from what occurred (sadness, anger or fears) nor be too arrogant if/when our adversaries try to kiss-ass and stroke egos because this only means that you've been identified by their intelligence as the potential weak-link (emotional-egotistical) to cozy up to.

Codes of Conduct "In General" should and shall be to respect one another despite any past rivalries our particular cliques might have had or could still be having because the world of incarceration supersedes the circumstances governing the outside hoods. Our codes of conduct do allow for circumstances of exception where cousins have significant reprobate issues that can't be squashed, they should be provided a place and space to dance it out and rejoin the ranks with respect for one another in place, leaving it behind. We shall, as a code of conduct, allow respect for our non-crip enemies as well. A trait exclusive to great men is tolerances as most things should be allowed to pass unnoticed between all cousins, between friends and particularly between enemies as a matter of practical wisdom because greatness is not easily disturbed or thrown off balance. It is however, important to keep a mental note of some of the more blatant attempts by an enemy to solicit a response so that once it becomes necessary to engage, our response will be appropriately thought out and measured for distribution at a time when its least expected, and perhaps in response to a much Much smaller infraction with an extreme and seriously disproportionate response.

We should and shall honor and enforce existing curfews set by the masses to allow late nights to remain solemn and quiet. We should and shall discipline our own folks we've determined as guilty of breaking protocols. We should not and shall not pretend or protect a loved one who has clearly transgressed and disciplines must remain stern so as not to facilitate favoritisms. We should and shall maintain our hygiene at all times and promote sufficient grooming. We should and shall maintain clean living quarters our personal bed area and/or camp lockers along with our photos, legal and miscellaneous paperwork and toiletries should and shall be arranged in a neat way to thereby command respect when K-9's are searching and to provide tell-tale security over our property if or when K-9's try to operate covertly as if they had not searched our belongings.

Every yard, camp unit or building of incarcerated loved ones should and shall maintain a kitty, a treasury or Crip store that is stocked with all the care package items to bless new arrivals and to issue an allowance to loved ones that are without funds or any means to sustain a viable incarcerated Crip lifestyle. In the absence of C-Team hood structures supporting a cousin, others should and shall take up the slack with pending inquiry to the squad and C.S.I. in the community nearest to the derelict cadre to be righteously reimbursed, given an opportunity to follow the Scriptures or shall provide reasoning why one of theirs has been abandoned. Incarceration is a serious situation and to abandon a Crip is a transgression never to be taken lightly.

Incarceration is a Situation #Nine

We abhor but endure the humiliation forced on us by this Imperial Nation

Who plagued us with such consternation through their Willie Lynch applications

Then after scores and years of annihilations, and millions of tears and argumentations

they begrudgingly balanced their trepidation, just barely yielding a bit on emancipation

As still today they cherish their confederation, but now a days is word plays of trickeration

for continuing black's death manifestation, using new tactics of dehumanization

Now attacking black's family visitations, and regulating to death black's communications

Successfully mobilizing the black depopulation, while our soldiers die strong in isolations

or in prison hospitals from nameless complications, and they dare us to yell race discrimination they'll deploy their media blacks with no hesitation, who slave to save their docile occupations

So we're come full circle to black strangulation, witnesses to our very own eliminations

the dirty knife to botch our own operation, I put it in a poem just to win your consideration

cuz once you read stuff, its hard to change the station, Incarceration is our #9 situation

Song: Situation #Nine

Inspired by. (Club Neuvo)

VII. The Faculty

"Therefore take up the whole armor of God, that you might be able to withstand in the evil day and having done all, to stand...therefore Stand!"
- Ephesians 6:13

Late one night in a cold cement dungeon in the notorious Pelican Bay - Security Housing Unit at California's Super Maximum Prison, an old comrade loses sleep trying to figure out where exactly in life had he and the cadré gone so wrong. Suddenly his usual nightmare transformed into a serene almost Buddha-like experience where various creatures of the land, sea and air began to communicate to him exactly where the Crips went wrong.

First an enormous American Flag colored Eagle explains that in raising her infants (much like raising an infantry) we must build the nest upon the highest heights and cliffs where no other creatures can reach or see. Her eaglettes come into the world knowing they are on top of the world and no other creatures exist above them. Eaglettes must first fight their way into the world because life's natural circumstance dealt them a hand much like the infantry where they are born in a hard shell that would confine them to death if they don't or won't break through it. The Mother Eagle finally concludes, "you've err'ed in allowing your impressionable infants/infantry to be born at such lows and so their thoughts and ambitions have acclimated below their highest potentials!"

Secondly the insect, a worker Bee chimes in explaining that although there are many freedoms with being able to soar above others, she prefers to live alot lower than the eagle but just within canopy-level of animals and/or people and her eggs come to life in the middle of high populace hives to learn their place in their cooperative structure from day one, participating in the natural cycle of pollinations, making honey and/or servicing the Queen. Then the Bee concludes that the Crips error is in: "Y'all egotistical desire to live in such unnaturally small cliques and in the misuse and abuse of your stingers even to your own demise.".

The third to interject is the deep voice of the a Gorilla who disagrees with both supposed freedoms of the ability to fly above folks but explained that in forming small, close-knit type communities all the female gorillas gladly participate in raising the band's infants as their own, daily grooming their fur and keeping constant eyes out for intruders. The African anthropoid ape insists adamantly that her infants much like the infantry had to be raised on the correct type of nourishments from day one otherwise as an always hungry adolescent, a youngster would resort to meat eating and ultimately cannibalism. The gorilla and her infants demonstrate how they are so much stronger than any of the meat eaters yet their diet is fundamentally (leaves berries, insects and worms) vegetarian. The female gorilla concludes confidently with a simple snort ""Y'all erred in allowing your infants/infantry to become cannibals!" then the huge ape disappears into the heavy foliage of the rainforest.

Fourth to arrive just as the sun begins to set, a huge Bengal Tiger emerges cautiously yet still confidently then offers a different perspective. She explains that her infants much like our infantry enjoys great refuge in being on the ground and finds great pleasure in eating meats, the tiger adds as a matter of factly, and this diet keeps them all very strong without turning them into cannibal type predators. However, she concludes, the most important lesson that our infants/infantry should have learned was to be invisible in our concrete jungles even while we are watching everything around us. So then, as she turns to retreat back into the tall grass and thickly hanging vines she says: "The greatest error you Crips continue to make is your arrogant and flamboyant ways which leave you vulnerable and open to all the scrutiny and attacks from any and all who despise you."

Fifth to arrive is the black panther emerging from the dark shadows, who is a supremely nocturnal predator to the core and agrees almost roundly with the words from the Bengal Tiger except that the panther has one particularly different approach which she has to share. Almost simultaneously low music begins like a score behind her words, an old hip hop song by Whodini called: "The Freaks come out at Night" softly sounds as the black Panther says: "It is my duty as a revolutionary to inform you that the greatest error you Crips continue to make is that y'all operate all hours of the day which defines you as menaces to society when actually yo' power and safety as well as the safety of yo' infants/infantry rests up under the blanket of the night..." she concludes "Remember that" and almost magically she disappears back into the cold dark night.

The Sixth arrival appeared like a huge screen at eye level, a magnificently illuminated facade of ocean blue water framed the face of a great killer shark who began to speak in perfect "hood" syntax: "Listen cousin, them punk-ass land dwellers don't know how shit goes in the real world, real talk, you gotta' be either prey or predator out here in the deep blue, ya'dig?!" The female shark swam methodically in a slow figure eight pattern as she continued "Be greedy! Live to eat, don't just eat to live, sometimes hiding and only sometimes riding, hell naw! That's for part-time predators who don't realize their off time is when they are the prey! And always keep it moving cuz, forever forward because if ever I stop or move backwards, I'll drown out here! We're proud of y'all up there giving the land-dwellers the blues, your mere presence strikes fear in the hearts and minds of the civilians whenever y'all smell blood just like we do and y'all dont even have your dorsal fin on display but still they know how that red stuff sends us and y'all into a frenzy. The only mistake we believe intimately hinders y'all infants/infantry's growth is that you're living too far from home so come on back down here to the deep blue and let's feast together" she concludes with a parting facial expression that could've passed for a smile and then she disappeared into the abyss.

Finally the Seventh vision appears, the very wisest reptile on the planet arrives, a giant old Sea Turtle slowly tracks from the water to the shore then begins in an equally slow old raspy tone "My child... My dear Crip children" she says "I too, like the Eaglettes, was born in an egg and had to fight my way into this existence we call Life, also I've swam amongst the predators in the oceans and the seas just as surely as I have had to hunt for my prey on these dry lands. Only the strong survive and I have survived it all so that now finally you, our great homosapien decendants could see your way back to us, even us all for holy counsel. You want and need to know of the secrets we each possess and by this You, our young Crip Nation have just declared to the outside world and the Universe your true intention to survive and so, You Shall! The old turtle paused for a moment and in Buddha-like-fashion began again: "A man who bows in the six directions does not do so in order to escape from external misfortunes. He does it in order to be on his guard to prevent evils from arising within his own mind." (Note: See: Practical guide to true way of living #1. Family life-The Teachings of Buddha), the turtle continues: "Your greatest error would be for you; the infantry to only choose some or one of our styles without embracing them all. You must fine tune and tailor them to fit your context as you certainly have tremendous trials up ahead and in order to prevail you shall certainly be required to incorporate and flawlessly exhibit all our styles at given times." The turtle suddenly turns away as if to leave, 'but wait!" almost jolted himself awake and out of his informative dream "What is the particular style I shall incorporate from you?" The huge turtle stops then looks back with piercing diamond blue gem eyes and said "but of course young cousin, mines is the most important of them all and the most obvious... Self security!" and immediately it disappears.

'Therefore take up the whole armor of God that you
might be able to withstand in the evil day and having done
all to stand... therefore stand!'

THE Holy Faculty - Ephesians 6:13

This faculty is the Holy Faculty perfectly designed and scientifically constructed of nine different but equally important parts. There are no parts that are unnecessary, there is nothing herein that we can do without. These carefully measured ingredients which you now have the honor and privilege of gathering are precise and absolutely critical in every detail. This is due in part to the enormity of the various cadrés and the whole Nation world wide whom each and every one shall also be maintaining this duplicate Blue printed structure knowing that it bonds us all together. Any alterations or substitutes shall serve as the red flags alerting all the True Blues that a community of imposters are in our midst and bringing shame to the game.

In life everything has an order, everyone and everything has a place even as the law of nature demands of everyone and everything to be moving, either growing stronger and evolving into more or rather slowly growing weaker and deteriorating into nothingness.

Those of us excellently committed to this C-Nation are obviously and absolutely still on the rise no longer splitting into angry cliques feuding because a killer and the folks in his crew had to prove themselves to that crew of squabblers they lost a fight to or becuz some baller pays one crew to clear out some other baller's crew holding a lucrative dope street. As we stick to Script we recognize that The Nation is ultimately a vehicle made up of multiple parts and components which although they are strong and sophisticated enough to survive on their own have all indeed heeded the call from nature to evolve now because surviving is no longer enough, this C-Nation intends to excel therefore this is the holy faculty by which we shall naturally get it done even excellently. A democratic assemblage of 1 or all 3 triumvirates from each team constitutes a legitimate faculty process.

Any of these gatherings where at least one triumvirate each of the nine teams are present shall constitute a legitimate Faculty (Blue Room) Meeting. Each cadre, hood or community should have at least one secure room with blue painted walls and a round table large enough to seat nine comfortably. In the rare occasions where the full 27 faculty members are attending then an outter layer of the other two triumvirates shall be seated behind their head triumvirate member thereby forming the Holy nine triangles. Faculty meetings all require maximum security to what degree the C.S.I. team deems necessary according to the social seasons and atmospheres of the day as well as the meeting's location. The entire Nation's Holy nine shall be titled and nic-named as follows so that if/when any one of the multiple cadres of the world should encounter another, we can relate and identify each other even excellently. The teams functions and triumvirate titles follow. #1. The Booting and Recruiting Team (The Squad), #2. The Arms Team (The Heat), #3. Crip Security and Informations Team (C.S.I./The Temperature or The Tempo.), = The Consortium Triangle of "Love". #4. Travels and Communications Team (Tray-Com or The Walkway Team), #5. The Treasury (The Pulse) #6. The Investments and Fundraisings Team (Capital Hill), = The Consortium Triangle of "Life". #7. The C-Team (Body and Soul), #8. Assignments and Education (Ass.-Ed. or Boot Camp), #9. The Strategy and Defense

Team (Noodles), = The Consortium Triangle of "Loyalty". All "9" teams shall function together as our Holy Crip Government allowing the team consensus and Faculty votes to define and direct each powerful cadre's forward motion and by design, each of the "3" consortium triangles shall operate closer and more consistently together due to their particular crafts. However, Every Crip world wide who represents the C-Nation each share in common The Commitment to Excellence with that True Blue Love, for Life, through Loyalty so, our Holy Faculty nor these triangles shall divide us but merely assigns most to serve in the capacity most suitable to ones natural potentials.

The Booting and Recruiting Team (The Squad) shall be an assemblage of the rough and toughest Crip goons the natural brawlers, street fighters, mixed martial arts and boxing specialist who love the homies, the Community, the Scriptures and laws as much as they love the taste of their own blood in their mouths. The Crips and Criplettes of this elite fraternity/sorority must love their commitment to excellence, discipline and family values even more than they love themselves because as enforcers of Death before Dishonor upon such a cut throat community (as most are) being altruistic is the order of the day, everyday.

The booting and recruiting team, the Squad is the very first fraternity in this triangle of Love and appropriately so because they are the main architects of pain (and love is often a by-product of pain.). These arbiters of painful disciplinary issuances are also the decision makers for our initiations into this great world of love. It's identical to the beautiful process of natural child birth. The pain a mother feels during labor always melts into love the moment that newborn takes that breath of life. Love and Pain often goes hand in hand even as it is only those we love the most that possess the power to hurt us the deepest. There will always be love in the world and there will always be pain so it is often the few and the True who can reconcile with the matrimony of the two. Most mainstream fraternities, sororities and serious secret societies engage in their own rituals of hazings, initiations or humbling thresholds and seasons of slave-like services to the collective "big brothers" because they've learned about the matrimony of Love and Pain. Most military branches turn a blind eye to harsh boot camp protocols, tattooings, brandings and piercings that date back to the mighty Zulus and even the Egyptians. It has become an underlying fact that methods of pain produce love and drives off the weak and cowardly.... "Not everyone who avoids getting initiated in, is a coward but All cowards try to avoid getting initiated in!" - A.K. Shakur. (Booting and Recruiting-Squad of South Central L.A.-1987).

There will always be angles or excuses one can make for why his or her initiation isnt necessary, however for those determined to be "Tried and True!" the initiation shall only last between 30 seconds to 3 minutes max. depending on the fraternity, on whether its three on one or a head up type of ring-regulated initiation, each cadre's own squad shall decide. Each cadré, each Crip community, each hood shall have three senior members from their team to serve on their faculty and represent each of the nine teams. Although this Booting and Recruiting team is made up of the roughest, the toughest and most gifted fighters of the hood, and although this team serves as the Crip law enforcement even they shall adhere to Faculty decisions and enforce them wholeheartedly. These most elite cousins of ours are absolutely the most violent and the most feared but they must also be the most loyal and able to reign in their own tempers. The faculty will often provide the case factors and the democratic consensus on the verdict with the Squad's triumvirates but then the disciplinary process and its severity will usually be negotiated and deliberated on by this team and their triumvirates alone. These three heads are: One Supreme Crip Judge and two Crip Magistrates who shall themselves and their team, take in the recommendations of merit from the community at large & then decide what allegations they will refer to the C.S.I. team for investigations or what goes to the faculty seeking a serious verdict. The Squad is not obligated to seek verdicts for small infractions which might only require them to issue intimidating warnings or/and mild body penalties (getting punched on from the neck down) but whenever head shots are to be administered and/or severe body penalties (getting hit with a bat or chain to break bones or slaughter) then the blue room should be notified to rule on it. The blue room is any legitimate faculty meeting where each team is represented therefore a gathering of "9" minimum to "27" maximum (whether telephonic, electronic or in person) constitutes a Faculty process/Blue room meeting where the consensus is the law and order of the day. This Booting and Recruiting team does the enforcing.

Additionally the obvious business of Booting folks from the hood and/or Recruiting new folks into the hood is their calling. The Squad is one of the most feared teams in the whole Cadre because when these brawlers hit the scene no one knows if an issue is about to be handled regarding someone getting the boot, if someone is on deck to be disciplined or if they are out scouting for recruits. No one knows but them and so its usually a better feeling to see the Squad going than coming. Furthermore, this vicious fraternity should have Criplettes within their ranks due to the reality of Love, Life and Loyalty because females sometimes slip up too and it would only be best if a crew of gritty females were at the ready to administer to their homegirls whatever disciplines, whatever bootings and whatever recruitings that need to be done. There are a whole host of dirty manual labor type jobs that need to be done in the cold underworld and this Booting and Recruiting team is "The Squad" the Crips rely on.

The Arms Team/The Heat is the second team within this particular trio's consortium triangle and it shall be an assemblage of Crips who are calm, cold & calculating (Triple C-status) because whenever they are called upon, that means that their cousins, the Squad could not remedy a situation manually and that alone is saying alot because 95% of our situations should and shall be resolved at some level short of calling in the heat. The heat team is one of the most secret fraternities of them all and once a Crip or Criplette is initiated, only then will he or she have some knowledge as to how they operate and where they operate from. This team has the elite triumvirates titled: (one) Marksman Master Sergeant and (two) Gunnery Sgt.'s for whom all intents and purposes must know their team inside and out before issuing any assignments and should each have their own caché located at a location they've deemed safe and secure. Each shall keep an inventory and log for their particular caché but must commit to memory the addresses. This team shall live and breathe Excellence by frequenting shooting ranges and mastering their particular tool (be it knives, a mace, fire arm or crossbow etc...) better than any other and then be graded based on performance, ability and temperament. This particular triangle of fraternities are meritoriously the Nations law enforcement which often requires most often the attitudes of a stickler as they shall push, pull and promote the quality disciplines of Love, Life, and Loyalty excellently.

The Crips and Criplettes of this Armory fraternity, (The Heat team) are extremely calm and disciplined and should regularly enjoy their own quiet moments for deep meditation even as they often deport themselves like Buddhist monks of the cadre, their discipline and quiet humility is intimidating to all:

> "As a knight guards his castle gate, so one must guard
> one's mind from dangers outside and dangers within; one
> must not neglect it for a moment. Everyone is the master
> of himself, he is the oasis he can depend on, therefore,
> everyone should control himself above all...
>
> The sun makes the day bright, the moon makes
> the night beautiful, discipline adds to the dignity of a
> warrior; so quiet meditation distinguishes the seeker for
> Enlightenment."
> - The Teachings of Buddha (IV. Sacred
> Sayings #6.)
> The Way of Practical Attainment.

In such cold times, living such cold lives, caught up in our cold rivalry and our cold love/hate relationships all while learning how to be cold blue blooded enough to weather the ghettos coldest storms in our Nation full of seriously cold mutherfuccas I suppose its only right to know there's always The Heat team near by who we can turn to because between real life and real death, who knows which is coldest...

> "Happy is he that always hath the hour of his death
> before his eyes and daily prepares himself to die."
> - Thomas á Kempis (1379-1471)

> "Although this Heat team is duty bound in our lives
> to protect and to serve, it is not because we have fear in
> life or death but our concern is to never experience or

exonerate dishonor! This team enforces our creed: "Death Before Dishonor!"".

- Diamond R. Phillips

"We cannot too greatly deplore the blindness of men who do not want to think of death, and who turn away from an inevitable thing which we could be happy to think often. Death only troubles carnal people."

- Francois Fénelon (1651-1715)

"Considering the certainty of death can provide a dynamic approach to life"

- Our Daily Bread
(Dec. 31st 2012)

In the times of old, there was a particular tool known to society as the "Peace Maker" and this tool's job was always clear, it would compel folks to "make" peace or "Rest" in it, ironically the peacemaker was the gun. This team is to us the official peacemaker we Love and Live by with Loyalty, however there is that most important safety mechanism which we must always keep in place on this gun and that is our oh so holy C-faculty. The Arms shall never be discharged without faculty authorization or eminent dangers and security threats there of because of this team's Triple C status of being calm, cold and calculating. Nevertheless, don't get it twisted, any one of these holy Crip Script enforcers of the law might under certain cold circumstances in this extremely cold world suddenly have to make a calm, cold and calculating decision heat checking some particular snowballs until they melt. Then these cousins with their triumverates, while knowing they shall be held accountable must now make the case that supports and justifies their actions which were so fast and unilaterally necessary with respects to satisfying the law of Love, Life and Loyalty. So then to repeat... 95% of our situations should and shall be resolved at some level short of calling in the heat and faculty (Blue Room) authorization is required before the heat is discharged because Crip force is lethal and should never be our 1st resort, we have evolved and shall only consider it last. For there is this one rule in Life that we know better than anyone else ever could...

If you live by the gun then so shall you die by the gun, Period!!!

Our C.S.I., the Crip Security and Informations team is the third of this three team consortium triangle and thus in conjunction with them (The Squad and the heat) this team is also about the business of Crip law enforcements. This C.S.I. is more commonly known as: "The Tempo," or the temperature team for they protect and serve the Nation by always knowing and controlling the hood's temperature inside and outside of the rank and file faculty. C.S.I. must be an assemblage of the type of cousins that knows everybody's name and everybody's business, even while they themselves maintain their integrity as our most clandestine "Blue-operations" team that keeps their own mouths sealed shut. The Triumvirates of this secret fraternity are: one Crip Watch Commander, one Sr. Director of Security and one Senior Director of Informations. These three shall excellently communicate with one another and their perspective members inorder to accurately reflect the consensus of their team in their "Findings" and "Recommendations" to the Faculty. Crip Security and Informations (The Tempo) Team shall keep files on individuals in the community and all the local businesses, schools and churches so that they have a knowledge of the Norms within their own community, even if it's merely a line or two describing the main street merchants during rush hour or a local church in financial trouble behind in repairs. This teams specialty is all about "knowing" what the temperature is in their world. These consummate security and information Crips are aware that their service is the most important of all because of course everything we do individually and especially collectively shall require security around it. We've danced in every dark corner around the world and only because our security is so excellent that we've managed to remain safe. Also, however... the most important component to maintaining safety and Security is the possession of information! As it is said..."Information is power" and so the cadré damn sure better have the power as we live this ghetto fabulous Crip life. Our Blue room-faculty meetings shall submit requests for C.S.I. to process and produce "Findings" and "Recommendations" on, then their "F's and R's" shall largely set a framework of Security based on the information that they gathered and recommend ways to move forward on the Cadrés agenda within that safer and more informed framework. This is the fundamental mechanism of this fraternity which trickles down and advises our every step and each breath we take. Everything from securing any locations where our faculty members meet, to securing venues where the cadré want to have a function or small party celebration; this team has the job of being informed about possible hostilities in other hoods, states and countries where a loved one is vacationing or where the cadre plans to do business and a great variety of other Security components.

The first Crip triangle consortium, (The Squad, The Heat and The Tempo.) is absolutely our altruistic triangle of "LOVE"! For us, "Love" is our very first and most valuable instrument. The works of these three fraternity teams in harmony is an instrument of Love like no other and an ingrained commitment to excellence which makes this instrument of ours, far more superior than all others. In: "the Force Theory" one Friedrich Engels famously argued that superior force and arms is what determined the Economic order and all the world powers.

> ... So, then, the revolver triumphs over the sword; and this will probably make even the most childish axiomatician comprehend that force is no mere act of the will, but requires very real preliminary conditions before it can come into operation, that is to say, instruments, the more perfect of which vanquish the less perfect; moreover, that these instruments have to be produced, which also implies that the producer of more perfect instruments of force, vulgo arms vanquishes the producer of the less perfect instrument, and that, in a word, the triumph of force is based on the production of arms, and this in turn on the production in general - therefore on 'economic power', on the 'economic order', on the material means which force has at its disposal." - F. Engels, Anti-Dühring
> New York International Publishers

This first triangle, Our Nation's triangle of Love is a tried and truely Superior instrument that remains totally selfless and in constant service for our advancement and so we must always return to them this high level of Love by deferring and consulting, by contributing information both great and small so that they can put the pieces together and finally by accepting the pains they might inflict on us for we know that only real love, only true and absolute love happens -via- pains. (Child-birth, defloration, cadré initiation and eulogization) Let us never forsake or fear love, let us never evade or avoid Love and most of all, let us never, never ever doubt love, deny love or dishonor love. This booting and Recruiting team, this Crip Armory team and this Crip Security and Informations team make up this, our first triangle consortium and this is our triangle of Love...

Travels and Communications (Tray-Com) or "The Walkway" team is the fourth of the Holy Nine but is also first with the cadrés triangle of Life. This team shall be an assemblage of each cadrés most personable and charismatic Crips and Criplettes. Tray-Com, better known as the Walkway team serves in the most dangerous capacity of all the teams because this fraternity is duty-bound with the task of representing the Nation and their particular hood outside of the safety of their own community. This teams central task is to establish safe and lucrative paths, i.e. "Walkways" into and throughout other hoods, communities, states and countries. The three head-Triumvirates of the Tray-Com team shall be named/ranked: one Commander, one Admiral and one Sr. Pilot. These three while working cooperatively with one another must adhere to their hood's blue room Faculty vote and agenda. Destinations and assignments shall have the benefit of each team's expertise as the assignments are drawn up so that travelers security triumvirates of this team. The triumvirates of this team each command on different terrain (Land, Sea and Air) and should interject when information is being missed (INRE: e.g. state lines, sea ports, passports, etc...) this thereby allows the faculty to assess the situation excellently.

The Crips and Criplettes of this team although personable and charismatic are still Crips and their well being is sacred to us in the highest order therefore when traveling to areas within or near another Crip or Ally's territory, city, state or country they must be notified and perhaps even consulted so that it is clear to them that a loved one is in their vicinity and they will be held accountable for those holy Crip souls. Furthermore, if/when a cousin from some other city, state or country (sticking to the Script) notifies us that their Tray-Com is coming to town we shall consult and (depending on if they are visiting or conducting business) we shall determine if cuz requires an escort, some armor or an advisement alert telling him or her that the travel plan should be aborted.

The Walkway team is as vital to us as was the explorers who reached the Americas on behalf of their hometown royalty. This team is a source of life and thusly make up the first team of our triangle of Life. They need not locate a land for us to pillage or steal because our dignity and honor is True Blue and Crip is already everywhere, Tray-Com need only provide a path for us to Crip walk down, establish communications on and to live by.

Travels and Communications operates not just as our instrument for creating walkways towards a better life in the civilian world but these cousins also serve as ambassadors of the underworld on behalf of the C-Nation who controls its life as well. We are the very air that the underworld breathes and life... real "Life" constitutes some sorta' movement biologically or metaphysically that confirms its existence. Fortunately for us, Tray-Com is mandated to move on our behalf in only a forward motion, despite the fact that hood life means we are born on a backwards flowing conveyor belt that empties into the graves and the gutters, into poverty and prisons we have a way forward, we have this the Crip Walkway we must rely on. What's unfortunate is that most folks within the higher tax brackets, the folks from the civilian world with stability and secure family values & with dynamics that usher them forward through life they tend to assume we have the choices and opportunities (like they've enjoyed) & that we simply choose to squander them all, sometimes deliberately, sometimes ignorantly even because we lack the will... us, we lack the will to push, pull, strive, us... we lack the will to fight and to live, how absurd! So now, finally its scripture that against all odds and against the backwards pulling momentum of that ghetto conveyor belt we're born on, we must and we shall stubbornly keep striving and pressing hard with the strong will of a Nation. The ambassadorship of Tray-Com is our vehicle of life building even more new bridges of life worldwide becuz the Crip Nation certainly has the will and everybody knows that where there's a will...there's a Walk way!!! Let no man or woman ever underestimate or devalue the importance of this team for it was just this sorta' team (but much smaller and much more ignorant) who first touched the Caribbean Islands in 1492-1503 being misled by Columbus believing they'd traveled all the way around the globe and hit India so he called it the West Indies and the natives, Indians. The Walkways he opened up (and the many others) produced a whole new world of unmeasurable "Life", wealth, and sadly death but our cadré isn't so evil and morally bankrupt (as they proved to be) so then the Tray-Com we send seeks only life and perhaps wealth, not death! We communicate Love, Life and Loyalty as we Cripwalk into new lands and are hereby forbidden to visit death upon any hood, state, country or island that welcomes us and embraces life, however...to threaten or harm Crip "Life" might bring on the rain. Life is precious, Crip life is sacred, Faculty members life is Holy so respect the Will and the Walkway!!!

The Treasury Team (B.K.A. The Pulse) is the second team of the Second Triangle which is this triangle of Life. This team is and shall be an assemblage of the more established and Senior members of our Crip Community. The trustworthy and loyal local store owners, the smartly retired entrepreneurs and successful ghetto stars and such whom have done well for themselves and are no longer involved in any parts of the game or the hustle. The Treasury team is numerically counted dead center within the Holy nine but serves as the source of Life we all depend on. This secret elect is our dearly beloved treasure even our very heart. This is the vital organ located at the center of our chest which the outside world of life-takers would pray to be able to pierce. This is the master organ responsible for providing for us our pulse. Nothing is more important to us living our Crip Life than us having and maintaining a strong pulse. The Triumvirates responsible for Life shall be titled: one Senior C-B-Prez. (Crip Bank President) Emeritus, one Sr. Treasury Secretary and one Sr. Crip Vice President. These cousins of ours absolutely must live and embrace this life Emeritus in order that our funds remain free and clean from all and any "dirty" entanglements. This Secret fraternity shall be no bigger than what is necessary to closely monitor, consult and control our vitals at a safe and efficient operating level. These three levels ideally are: Crip Surplus, Crip Balance and Crip Deficit. Each of these levels shall have its own high dollar amount and low dollar amounts in place to distinguish how close or how far the Treasury is from where it wants to be or from where it once was. Each hood shall have its own Crip Balance which is an operational amount that accommodates its own regular expenditures (for that month/year) without falling into their deficit ranges. Each hood/ cadré shall have a healthy surplus to withdraw from before big projects can be entertained and approved by this team at our faculty meetings. The triumvirates and elite Crip accountants of this "Life" team must decide when funds are getting low and need to be replenished, they shall prepare a statement for the Blue Room faculty who will then negotiate a remedy all can agree upon. This team may propose hood dues to increase or to move from monthly to bi-weekly or the faculty might direct the fundraisers to sponsor some type of lucrative investment which will profit greatly and get us back into the green (Crip Surplus) range even reaching the high level where more investments can occur and put this Pulse team at ease. This Treasury Team is like our electrocardiogram (EKG) with the sole purpose of monitoring our Pulse/heartbeats and when we are in danger and way before we experience cardiac arrest that requires resuscitation these are the life savers who become the alarm. These cousins of ours are determined to maintain a steady pulse which ultimately became their hood name and although the Triumvirates are all on Emeritus status they can have several interned Crip accountants who are active in the cadre and more in tune with the hood atmosphere and occurrences. Each and every hood within the C-Nation shall have the very same Holy Faculty and Triumvirates but we all dont have the same amounts of money or personal incomes so each community should establish their surplus, their balance and their deficits at levels more proportionate to their tangible collective income. This team shall also establish their own hood's dues and the frequency in which it is paid so as not to unrealistically burden our own loved ones. From 50 cents per month to $50.00, its contingent on that hood's reality. Our accountants know that numbers do add up, so... a million Crips can give one dollar and it produces a million dollars that buys their community something that could become two million. Proposals for dues and penalty fines must never be oppressive however to sustain life in the name of our own Crip Love, Life and Loyalty we have to keep a healthy pulse for our heartbeat as our pulse plays the rhythm of Life, the blue'tiful sound we live by, the Crips song of "Life!"

The Investments and Fundraisings Team (B.K.A. Capital Hill) is the third team of the 2nd triangle consortium of "Life". This team is and shall be an assemblage of our sharpest and most "plugged-in" business minds. These are the brilliant younger Crips and Criplettes who follow stocks and bonds, who study real estate books and tax lien auctions while others stay current on commerce opportunities and Produce prices. The Investments and Fundraisings team does exactly what it says except in an assortment of "cutting-edge" ways. The three heads of this super-elite fraternity, the Triumvirates are titled: one Chief Executive Financier, one Executive Coordinator of Investments and one Executive Coordinator of Fundraisings. These holy cousins of ours shall be the ones whom we challenge to make things happen in our Faculty Meetings. Money is of vital importance to real life and so, when the team monitoring our vitals say its low (The Pulse) then this team must create or make a way. This team is appropriately better known to most as: Capital Hill, (not Capitol) because this is where all capital ventures are executed from. This team must be diverse in their interests and fields of expertise because Life requires it, investing and raising funds requires it and capital (i.e. money) almost certainly demands it. The Crips and Criplettes of this team should have vision and aspirations but are duty-bound through Love, Life and Loyalty to this team's consensus along with their triumvirate's democratic decisions on how to move forward on a project. However, the visionaries must be heard and all their legitimate aspirations shall at least be considered/reviewed. Capital Hill shall have a place or residence from which to operate safely, conduct research, study and to have their own Three team consortium meetings on behalf of their "Life" triangle even as if functioning as the Cadré's legislative branch over all things money. Therefore The Walkway, The Pulse and The Capital hill shall consort together as our community's triangle of Life and on behalf of Life shall legislate blue prints for making money. Their Blue print legislations however, must be presented to the Blue room faculty for passage, even as their legislative proposals might employ or impede on the other teams. These Blue prints decided upon at Capital Hill are like legislation passed by the civilians Capitol hill because our Capital Hill and this triangle consortium of "Life" is altruistically divine, supremely unselfish and good therefore their proposals can rarely be denied. Life is a precious and most perfect gift and these self-less Crips are truly our custodians of Life! One Love, One Life, One Loyalty!!!

The Crip Teamsters or The C-Team (B.K.A. Body and Soul) is our seventh team of the holy Nine but our first team within the consummate Triangle of Loyalty. This team shall be an assemblage of special Crips and mostly Criplettes who are dependable and hold a great capacity of Crip honor and compassion beyond what most other Crips can comprehend. These Crip goddesses of ours are tasked with the single-most important duty of all others as this, The C-Team shall care for the incarcerated and confined cousins whom were put in far away locations designed to make the average loved ones forget. This team is far above average and shall be honored and acknowledged regularly.

The C-Team shall be a host of women and men with clean arrest records and preferably have a specific loved one in confinement somewhere, e.g. (a baby-daddy, father, brother, mother, sister or child) which thereby brings him or her into the high knowledge of how important this service is. These altruist Crips are the keepers of the community's "Body and Soul", the confined bodies and lost souls of cousins that served faithfully and are incarcerated but still representing all of us honorably. Cousins such as these must never be abandoned, not purposely nor negligently as it becomes their whole hood's transgression, violating the Crip Scriptures nefariously in the eyes of Love, Life and Loyalty. To prevent such a travesty every hood (Crip Community) must establish this team with a home as a headquarters to operate from, a paid phone line to accept collect calls, a van or appropriate modes of transportation to visit our incarcerated and run errands for the loved ones who can't do it themselves. This C-Team shall bare no expenses upon themselves such as rent for the headquarters, utility bills, costs for supplies and correspondences and it is often smarter and equitable for everyone that headquarters be established at the homes of elderly mothers and hood grandparents left behind by one of our incarcerated cousins. The incarcerated Crips are often the central breadwinners of their household and thusly leave behind their dependents (children, baby's mommas and/ or younger siblings) who might otherwise suffer if they don't become part of this C-Team. This collective is the only team of the holy nine who has "Blue Ribbon" status. This means that their requests shall never be denied. Being keepers of our beloved confined Body & Souls is so Royal and True Blue of an occupation that a homegirl or homeboy serving on their hood's C-Team shall be able to discreetly select any comrade for a tryst unless some great and unusual circumstance exists which a faculty Triumverate from any one of the Holy Nine must verify in order that an apology can be articulated with the denial. In general C-Team members should be granted their every request yet our C-Teamsters shall not abuse or dishonor their Blue Ribbon status but in the name of love, life and loyalty these cousins do have needs and their needs must take precedence over ours who are free.

Incarcerated cousins shall not jeopardize the sanctity of any headquarters by involving that location with any unauthorized business deals. The Cadre having a place of residency which is absolutely untainted is mandatory and critical to everyone's future. The C-Team's headquarters is the Cadre's think tank especially because the minds of our incarcerated cousins become nothing short of brilliant and simply overflowing with highly innovative and lucrative ideas which are constantly at the disposal of this particular team. These loved ones we all know as our "Body and Soul" is in fact the first team in complete authority on the concept of Loyalty. However, in the periphery of all that they know and do in the name of loyalty the C-Teamsters still see this world for what it is and with real eyes, realize, real lies are being perpetuated by such a hateful system (Courts, Peace Officer's Unions and Crime Victims groups) to taint and turn off folks human emotions of compassion, empathy and forgiveness for the less fortunate and uneducated bodies and souls that make up our communities and shanty towns. We understand and through this C-team overstand even clearer now, the concept and dynamic of American Capitalism simply by studying schematically the common school ground apparatus called the seesaw where, in order for one side to prosper and stay positioned up high, the other side has to fail and stay positioned low. And so this has been ever since the inception of the Americas. Millions had to be anchors wedded to horrible lows so that smaller thousands could snatch up lands and rule nations from up high. 1st was slavery, then corrupt "prisoner leasings" that proved to be worse than slavery, then came the Reconstruction era that qualified hate and naturally led to Jim Crow laws articulating superiority which society (the Courts and the media) all agreed on until the civil rights era made Americans expose themselves -via- Television to the world forcing them to act/play ashamed. How could America continue to prosecute the crimes of the Third Reich against Europe's Jews- -via- the media footage when America's own footage of hate was the top story worldwide? Very quickly American hate had to take on a super subtle and shrouded form so the child conceived in the 1930s was born in the 1950s and named: "Law and Order". The rhetoric of Mass Incarceration which is now society's common thought (and greatest evil) flourishing by the mid-to-late 1980's in California and across the U.S.A. by devouring the "Body & Souls" of The Crips even as visits were harassed, discouraged and ultimately family visiting was out-lawed in a subtle homage to genocide (procreation versus Safety and Security rhetoric). So, for the Cadré, our C-Team are the heaven-sent guardians over our Body and Soul, our confined loved ones to comfort them and with their Blue Ribbon status care for them (the incarcerated) because Love inspires it, Life requires it and Loyalty admires it..

The Assignments and Education team (Ass. Ed. or Boot Camp) is our eighth team of the holy Nine and second within this altruistic "Triangle of Loyalty". There is no greater or more important representation of any hood than that hood's own Ass. Ed. because this is the foundation from which we all emerged. Assignments and Education is exactly what it says, this team gives all Crips and Criplettes the assignment he or she is naturally best suited for, the assignment he or she will Love and Live with Loyalty for. The assignment to serve and be recognized throughout the entire Crip Nation and respected world wide. However, these extremely huge and important assignments can only be issued through education and Boot Camp is duty-bound to teach and educate every Crip and Criplette about all nine disciplines.

It is perfectly normal for a loved one to enter boot camp already intent on being suited for and assigned to a particular team's roster but nobody tells Boot Camp what to do or how to do it. Faculty members may however, make recommendations to boot camp members and these recommendations shall absolutely be considered due to Love, Life and Loyalty as we know that we're all working together to achieve the very same final outcome which is: Excellence! A Crip having seen potentials of some kind in a particular young loc or new Boot camp inductee is obligated to transfer that helpful information to the proper authorities and Ass. Ed. is as proper as one can be. The Triumvirates of this most important team shall be titled: One Crip Principal/Colonel and two Lieutenant Colonels, one as Vice Principal of Assignments and one Vice Principal of Education. The Lt. C - Vice Principal of Assignments shall be responsible for exams and the mobilizing of a team of dedicated cousins to examine the Boot Camp Crips and Criplettes thoroughly, on sticking to the Holy Scriptures and on the materials about each team as well as all recommendations from their Educators and personal sponsors so that the bootcamp inductees can be assigned. Any Crip or Boot Camp graduate can be reassigned to another of the holy nine if his or her skill set allows it or he or she can be completely "unassigned" and simply be a member of the hood (not the Cadré) and still represent Crip from the fringes if his or her skill set (or heart) is not up to par. This Assignments portion of Ass. Ed. must protect the Par!!!

So, while it is the duty of the Assignments department of Ass. Ed to protect this Par it is the duty of the Educations department absolutely to inspire and establish a set par. The Holy Crip's Par is one of Excellence, of Death Before Dishonor, and one of Love, Life and Loyalty and All Crips must be at least "up to Par"! Each team and/or consortium triangle will have their own Par for their teams own "Particulars" which are actually their team's own directional learning materials that specifically enhance whatever discipline or hood-serving objectives they're on. However, the purpose of Boot Camp is to at least summarily educate all of us on all nine of the Holy disciplines but more importantly it's where faculty Crips must explore our hearts and minds thoroughly in order to tap into, then cultivate each inductee's own personal gift/knack for any one of the nine team's particular functions one might have so that it can be confirmed (Tested) then ordained a skill-set. These Royal Blue Riders are faced with this most critical task and happily excel at it as "This" is their particular gift. Boot Camp's faculty members in both the Assignments and the Educations dept's all have a knack for seeing raw talent and unharnessed potentials and they love when an inductee displays an aesthetic taste for any one of the teams unique materials becuz then the educating and the assigning all flows seamlessly. The following are some movies which shall inspire and intrigue a cousin towards his or her most natural service: (1) Baby Boy, (2) Passion of the Christ, (3) Once Upon a Time in America (4) Scarface, (5) Warriors (6) The Godfather, (7) Drumline, (8) Black Rain, (9) Poetic Justice, (10) Prison Song, (11) Avatar These movies are among the most intimate messege movies we know and can draw our particulars from.

The shrewd Love triangle might have Heat members that particularly note the way Scarface had to be humbled at the end. Squad members might enjoy all the pure hand to hand combat displayed in the old movie classic Warriors, CSI, The Godfather, and all three enjoying "Black Rain" as our Asian consorts put it down. The Life triangles C-Team would sympathize with "Passion of the Christ", & "Avatar" being wronged by the govt. and "Prison Song". The Loyalty triangle would certainly embrace the theme of "Drumline", Noodles would enjoy Once Upon a Time in America and The Godfather. The Walkway and Capital Hill must study the mistakes made in Scarface, Black Rain and Godfather as our "Pulse" team takes notes. Ultimately All provide particulars for someone and Boot Camp should regularly show all of them and enjoy.

The Nine Holy Disciplines-Outlined.

Name	Job Description	Reading Particulars	Work/Learning Settings
The Squad	Mixed Martial Arts With Street Fighting	(1) Extreme Unarmed Combat by. (Martin J. Dougherty (2) "Monster" by. (Kody Scott)	Boxing Gym, Grassy areas, Dirt or Parking Stalls
The Heat	Weapons Specialists	(1) "The Ultimate Guide to U.S. Army Survival Skills, Tactics, and Techniques" by. (Jay McCullough) Skyhorse Publishing	Archery & Shooting Ranges Hunting expositions, etc...
The Tempo.	Blue Black Ops.	(1) "What every Body is saying: An Ex-F.B.I. agent's guide to speed reading People" by. (Joe Navarro/M. Karlins).	Home, Room, or offices where maps, files & info. can be readily consulted.
The Walkway	Foreign Affairs	(1) "The Art of Seduction" by. (Robert Greene)	House, room, or office where maps, files and info. can be readily consulted.

The Pulse	Banking/ Savings	(1) This "Holy Crips Bible"	"
Capital Hill	Revenue	(1) The Shadow Market by. (Eric J. Weiner) (2) The Prosperity Bible by (Napoleon Hill et. al.,) (3) "Free Money They don't want you to know about" by. (Kevin Trudeau)	
The "C-Team"	Write, Visit and Care for the Confined	(1) "A Taste of Power" by. (Ellaine Brown) (2) Assata by. (A. Shakur) (3) Book of Na'vi	House, Room, or Office -HeadQuarters- where phones take collect calls & Correspondence materials available.
Boot Camp	Educate and Ordain	All Books required by and conducive to the Holy Nine Disciplines.	Any house/apt. where three areas are divided to allow each triangle or team to learn.
Noodles	Think Excellently.	(1) "Think and Grow Rich" by. (Napoleon Hill) (2) 48 Laws of Power by. (Robert Greene) (3) Top Secret America by. (D. Priest/W.M. Arkins) (4) The Teachings of Buddha (5) The "5" Rings by. (Miyamoto Mucashi)	A room painted Blue with a large World map and a circular table able to seat "9" forming the Holy Faculty & Top Notch www.accessibility

There are well over a million Crips and Criplettes world wide, thousands of hoods and hundreds of cities, regions, islands, towns, government projects and apartment complexes where the cadre is poor and moralé is low but with these disciplines... we shall rise. In life, we joke, we clown and we learn how not to give a fucc about dying and by proxy we couldn't careless about living, but, by becoming serious about these disciplines... we shall live! We shall Love, for Life, with Loyalty!

> "Education is the kindling of a flame, not the filling of a vessel"
>
> > \- Socrates

> Any particular set or hood may expand and must evolve with these nine disciplines but none shall stray away or replace any one of them for it's a discredit to them all and to all of us being stalwart and true to the game.
>
> > \- Stanley "Tookie" Williams

Assignments and Education should have time and space set aside for each of the nine disciplines to be able to specifically concentrate and focus on their craft. If it be a Boot camp compound or an apartment divided into three areas fit for each triangle to share, somehow we must make it work. Even moreso, we must thrive in the direction of higher learning however we can, especially seeing how true quality education is being ever so subtly priced out of our reach. For us, this is where our baby brothers and sisters can pursue their G.E.D. at any age they choose. This team shall heavily favor their region, city or area's basic school curriculum and acquire all the materials necessary to teach it (but to our own) at least two or three years younger than their civilian peers get it at school. Ass. Ed. is made up of Crips that are devoted to putting us ahead of the rest of the world and as a family we have this holy team's commitment to see our youth prematurely educated as well. It is the true spirit of Loyalty that is always aimed at us as members that also extends to our own personal loved ones by proxy. This second and most critical team within the triangle consortium of Loyalty is duty bound to teach us all what Love, what Life and absolutely what Loyalty really means. This lesson we shall learn both by their deeds of determination and their mandate for us to fulfill "Bible-Study" i.e. "Sticking to the script"! Excellently!!!

Strategy and Defense is the third within this three team consortium triangle of Loyalty and ninth of the Holy nine disciplines of our altruistic Crip Faculty. This is the final most sacred team of every hood, community, tribe and cadré in the C-Nation. Strategy and Defense's nic-name is Noodles and serves as the excellently functioning brain of our body. Our Noodles team triumvirate shall operate under the titles: One Senior Crip Chairman of the Board and two vice-chairs as one Senior Architect of Strategy and One Sr. Minister of Defense to represent at Blue Room Faculty Meetings. Noodles as a whole must serve their particular hood's wants and needs, they must be stalwart about maintaining the progressive and ever-evolving agenda of their hood and balance it with the ever-present reality and conditions of the day. These gifted and chosen cousins must have the natural creativity and the drive necessary to make great conditions and situations out of the bad ones all around us. Even as God made man from the dust of the ground and called it good, these elite Crips and Criplettes shall make prosperity from the dirt of the earth so that we may call it good. So says the Dirt!

First there is strategy and under the Sr. Architect there are subordinates and junior architects who by definition are Mastering Strategy in one of these two capacities: #1. The science and art of military command aimed at meeting the adversary under conditions favorable to our cadre. #2. The careful planning and methods necessary to achieve the best end results! Due to the immensity of the Crips, our architects shall be faced with countless adversarial norms which they must resolve (e.g. Ethical norms, Social norms, Economical norms, etc...) because the Safety, Structure and Sustenance of the entire Crip Community depends on Noodles absolutely after wars have already settled the lines of demarcation. Physical battles and war is no huge challenge for the Crips in the Nation, our biggest challenges, our most frequent adversity comes in the form of everyday dilemmas and our obstacles being presented at Faculty meetings, these are what require strategy and defense. All ethical, social or economic matters must be carefully dealt with as though we're handling military matters in our Faculty meetings. Therefore Noodles shall approach every matter thoughtfully and apply their best strategy deliberately at the request of the Crip Faculty. Triumvirates from whatever team must present the specific matter to be dealt with and/or represent the consensus of their particular team at the Faculty meeting in either an oral fashion or a written statement. Any team's Triumvirate (head representative) may provide information, assistance or input orally or in writing in regards to resolving another team's problem as we are all just mere parts of the same body and duty-bound to contribute to the cadrés forward motion and progress. However, Noodles shall accept all the available information and input then provide the ultimate resolution at some later time or date. Great strategy requires careful deliberation authorized by the consensus of the strategy team members (especially in regard to complex matters) then scrutinized by the other half of this highly sophisticated team known as: Defense in order for the process to be complete. It's their job to scrutinize and be critical of all strategic measures.

> "Anything in life that is Righteous, True and Real
> shall be able to stand Scrutiny!!!"
>
>   - A. K. Shakur

The Defense portion of each cadrés Noodles team is burdened with becoming the standard by which all Strategy is tried by fire before it can be handed over as a true resolution for the Faculty. Our Senior Minister of Defense may have several subordinates as well as a Jr. Minister and Secretary of Defense to help rally their collective for the turned-up flames of scrutiny they regularly use to make strategies excellent. This side of Noodles should be as large and diverse as necessary but also MUST know the true and genuine nature of argumentation and discourse. All triumverates and faculty members would do well to know and practice correct argumentation especially when dealing with another Crip. To keep it simple, argumentation/discourse is only a form of communicating back and forth ones thoughts or opinions regarding a subject, but then to know and practice its true nature we must be genuinely open to hear both sides of whats being discussed. Furthermore, in sticking to the Crip Script we all must understand the dynamics of any argument among our own involves a simple risk, the risk of being won over. Each and every exchange of ideas or opinions among Crips absolutely entail the same risks and it is only when we enter into an exchange unrealistically or disingenuously that arguments become fights or wars. This defense team reminds us that their applications of fire to our ideas only aim to turn them gold. Therefore the arguments and passions that happen among a team and/or its triumvirates are only the furnace purifying their collective opinions into one solid gold nugget (as their consensus) and likewise, the arguments and passions that will happen among the hoods faculty meetings is also the sort of smelting process of all the holy nine consensus ingredients to form a final gold bar, tried and true. None of these refining processes shall be taken personally, rehashed outside the circles or in any way weaponized against a loved one (or ally) mentioned in the discourses.

> II Timothy 2:20-21 "In a great house there are not only vessels of gold and silver but also of wood and clay, some for Honor and some for dishonor. Therefore if anyone cleanses himself from the latter, he will be a vessel for Honor... (sanctioned and useful for the master, prepared for every good work)".
>
> - The Holy Bible

This ninth and final team completing fully, the holy triangle of Loyalty and also bringing to completion the entire Crip Faculty is our highest, most important function absolutely because this is our brain, our Noodles, our holy Strategy and Defense team and they alone are burdened with the duty to do our strategizing for the betterment of all nine teams and the advancement of the entire Crip Community as well as excellently defending each and every team's own service to the hood/community through studying details and refining only what may need to be refined under the scrutiny of Blue Room Faculty Meetings.

It is because the Crips have no Kings or Dictatorships that our Faculty Meeting's discourse functions as our perfect democratic instrument to fix and/or resolve anything broken or problematic that we shall face. The huge obstacles and complex trials that trip up and topple the lesser governments and corporations shall not defeat the Crips. The sure signs of healthy Crip social spheres are visible in those hoods capacity to engage in critical discussions, to identify and appraise problems and proposals and to always be able to stand under scrutiny. Our beloved defense portion of the Noodles team provides that scrutiny in this simple form, they always ask the right questions and are always compelling us to have back-up plans. In the name of Love, Life and Loyalty we must allow Noodles to "lead" in the area of strategizing and defending all parts of each of those strategies by simply asking: "But, what if that doesn't work???".

Applying such a simple question to a proposed strategy does one of two things: it reveals an excellent answer or it compels contingencies (i.e. Back up plans) over and over until excellence is satisfied.

> v. "But avoid foolish and ignorant disputes knowing
> that they generate strife"
>
> — 2 Timothy 2:23v.

Each and every hood's own Noodles team being able to function as a whole and be so critical of its own strategies is what guarantees excellence and providing such excellent counsel for the benefit of their community, this is our definition of Loyalty. It is these Holy Nine disciplines all grounded in Love, in Life, and Loyalty that makes us superior to civilians, to enemies and our own cousins from other hoods who have not yet gotten themselves "Crip Ordained" by sticking to the Script.

So, in conclusion and absolutely like the mother eagle, the bee, the gorilla, the tiger, the black panther, the killer shark, and the giant turtle, each and every one of our disciplines are superior in their own uniqueness and at their own particular crafts/services to their hood. Each and every Crip life (body and soul) is a most precious jewel to us especially once he or she gets ordained and this status shall stretch Nationwide to and fro every hood or community sticking to the Script. Establishing and joining this Crip faculty makes us know who we are as individuals and collectively, it produces great purpose and reveals one's greatest potential and in so doing we meet prosperity along the way.

> Knowing who you are Really, and knowing your role
> only makes your role that much more clear and easier to
> establish as fulfilled which in turn is the main quality that

makes you so valuable to any and every team within your faculty. For our valuable and holy Blue flag members, we shall move heaven and earth to honor, to protect and to serve so by All MEANS... stick to the holy Crip Script!

"All Scripture is given by inspiration of God and is profitable for doctrine, for reproof, for correction, for instruction in righteousness"

- 2 Timothy 3:16

The Faculty Facilitation

All major disasters, disruptions or deadly occurrences such as blackouts, hurricanes, earthquakes, riots or even invasions from some foreign entities will call forward the strongest and will certainly collapse the weak. We obviously have proven our ability to excel under any and all of these circumstances yet here is an example of our faculty, our holy nine disciplines and essentially our Community Raised Infantry Progressing. On all cylinders... Full Throttle!!!

Immediately a meeting is called for the Full Faculty to gather at their cadrés Blue Room or whatever available rendezvous location they might be able to tightly secure based on whatever circumstances are at play. Three heads from each team shall be present even if last minute promotions become necessary to fill vacant seats. Every team must be represented in Emergency Full Faculty Meetings by three members of each team so that we can account for as much of whats going on with us and what needs to happen going forward, as is humanly possible. Finally its down to business!

At the round table or makeshift circle, Strategy and Defense begins by handing the lead to which ever team best suits the scenario: (e.g. Natural disaster hits the community hard, many are dead, Injured or homeless - <u>The Triangle of Life</u> is given the lead with their three team Consortium of Capital hill (to raise funds), the Treasury and the Travels & Communications team to blue print how everyone must pitch in to rebuild our community.) or if a disaster is visited upon us at the hands of police hate and rage, the Triangle of Loyalty has to take the lead. (e.g. several homes in the hood have been raided, charges have been trumped up on alot of key teams and/or their homes are no longer secure, The

Boot Camp team is immediately preparing to assign new recruits into those vacant positions and with new recruits comes new homes which can be newly secured. The C-Team gets immediately contacted by all our confined cousins who explain what they're being charged with and why so that our legal counsel can be contacted as well as those confined cousin's needs becoming immediately fulfilled. Meanwhile Noodles, our Strategy and our Defense can step up and do what they do best to keep the hood functioning smoothly.).

However, the instant example which shall be given here is an attack on several faculty members and their civilian family by an unknown entity as a means of intimidation:

The rains sprinkled down softly in even layers descending from the grey evening sky only to land quietly atop the car hoods and roof tops of the long train of limousines, Maybachs, Cadillacs, Lowriders and S.U.V.'s trailing slowly down the long winding cemetery road. The trees, the green grass and wet gravestones all seem to be standing silently at attention on both sides of the motorcade processional, all of them yielding to this sad moment where peace had obviously come just to be still. The body of a young female had been mutilated, set on fire then discarded on a residential sidewalk in a quiet upper class neighborhood, left smoldering like a heap of burnt trash that nobody wanted, that nobody loved, that nobody cared for but somebody was wrong. This innocent young girl was related to the Crips and so every drop of her precious blood that was spilled was to be repaid at a high price. Something sinister had crept up on her down in that City of Angels (which we better know as the city of no pity) and that something had nothing to do with the peaceful hood she was ditched in, this was someone's idea of making a statement and we got it loud and clear. Behind closed doors at the repast location, an impromptu meeting takes place resulting in a hood-wide: B.O.L.O. alert. "Be-On-Look-Out". This alert calls on all teams and folks within the community to open their eyes and ears. Crips already exist in a heightened state of alertness but during a B.O.L.O. everyone is endowed with a wealth of details from the smallest to the largest all of which are given to the triumvirates so that at faculty meetings one might be able to connect the dots.

The Triangle of LOVE becomes the primary in situations of our Crip Security. (The Squad-BKA The Booting and Recruiting team, The

Heat-BKA The Crip Armory and The Tempo. Or the temperature BKA Crip Security and Informations team.). Crip Love is aggressive and so this triangle is the most aggressive of all because when we have to call on Love everybody knows that Love hurts! Love is given the lead. Its routine protocol that when one of us has been harmed or even seriously threatened our intimidating Squad team will send some of their best brawlers into various establishments owned and/or frequented by old enemies (and every potential enemy) just hoping to flush out anyone's paranoia or suspicious (self-guilty) responses to their presence. When the Squad's rough and rugged goons C-walk into your world, your only smart recourse is to be honest and keeping it "one hundred" because our folks believe: "The Truth shall set you free!". The Squad usually serves in the "Hands On" capacity of: "To boot you, To recruit you, To protect you or to serve you" but in scenarios where information might be obtained the Squad will have at least one member of Crip Security and Informations (The Temperature) team available to by-pass all the physical persuasions a "cooperative" might want to avoid. Yet and still, there are those always looking to outsmart or out gangster the Crips and so, blue heaven forbid, these types of poor delusional souls who purposely don't or won't cooperate with our Squad-Temperature units, there's only one other team in The Triangle of Love for them to meet; Up from the firery pit of hell emerges the Heat. Unfortunately, the heat team don't carry no combustible note pads or plastic recorders So...it should be no surprise that the opportunity to provide the info. and honesty has passed. The Triangle of Love is duty-bound to keep all the haters at bay at any cost and in security situations where Crip lives have been lost, our blood spilled, our outer family's sanctuaries disturbed, you can believe the war between love and hate is apparent and in war the Crip Triangle of Love always conquers hate. (bye haters!).

A second faculty meeting is called within two weeks of the repast meeting. Everyone is eager to hear what the Triangle of Love has turned up because everybody has heard about how they'd been turning up all through the city, tapping on car's windows and knocking on folks doors causing even the most sinister of ghetto hoods to reach out to our Noodles team calling for reprieves from the investigative tours in exchange for collaborative meetings to possibly attack the culprits together. The three heads from each team in the triangle of Love confessed with heavy hearts that no definitive leads towards suspects or a motive had materialized but they vowed to press harder. Everyone knows the other's commitment to excellence is intact, not yet warranting any question so the meeting moves on. Each team briefs the faculty on any b.o.l.o. intel no matter how insignificant it may seem. Suddenly our ever impressive C.S.I. team-representatives connects the dots that nobody else was seeing. The Travels and Communications team (-BKA- The Walkway) just happened to mention that "3" huge business transactions in different states (but conducted with the same particular Latin corporation) were reported as being conducted under unusual duress. (e.g. Triple their amount of armed executives and gunmen rudely refusing to lower their assault rifles, etc...) This sort of turbulence alone doesn't even register on the Crip's scale as a threat because we are naturally just harder to frighten, but during a "b.o.l.o." this info added up, it mattered! Meanwhile, the hood's: Investments and Fundraisers team-BKA-Capital Hill have recently made some donations in Community Service to a couple of children who were chased out of school and stabbed up just for being black, attacked by their own schoolmates. Their parents parents were told (two different schools, two different kids, two different mothers crying hysterically) and all they could think to do was call up the Crips. All of this, plus our reliable C-Team (Our Body and Soul) learned from their steady stream of info. coming out of the various Institutions that Mexicans were trying to characterize themselves as: "at war" with the blacks. This information taken independantly usually would've been filed away but during a b.o.l.o. every tiny bit of information counts. Now C.S.I. decides that their recent encounters during their business transactions in other states could possibly be linked to these aggressions we're experiencing here. The final bit of data which would cause all of it to gel, would come from our own Latino triumvirates from: Travels and Communications (The Walkway Team) who had personally been the ones conducting them: "out of state" transactions which seemed unusually tense. One Puerto Rican, one Cuban, one Dominican explained: "It's possible that the Cartel may think they are at war with blacks on a racial basis but not on a business tip!" the white Cuban agreed as the fair skinned Dominican adds "They imagine themselves to be smarter than blacks and all other Latino people so... its possible that they'd engage in war-like activities in one city and then do business in another and think none of us the wiser". Finally a

Puerto Rican woman rises to her feet and says, "Listen everybody... none of us are interested in going to war with our own business connections but hey..." her pontificating begins as her golden fingers with ten perfectly manicured blue fingernails spread flatly on the wood finished faculty roundtable "After a dozen dances where I've handed those mutherfuccers a hundred and fifty gees, all of a sudden they're holding choppers to my head like we ain't come to do business?". Her voice rises as if it was a question but then it lowers as she says what they all knew was hanging in the air. "Naw cuz, they wasn't just being cautious, those mutherfuccers were guilty and they was scared!" Silence visits the faculty room for a moment. "So lets hit'em!" a triumvirate from the heat team suggest. "No! Excellence first!" a voice of reason from the Noodles triumvirate reminds us: "We're not sure until we get the details of the autopsy" as he looks directly at C.S.I. "We need to know if her hands were tied behind her back, okay?" (the deceased girl). As a result of the Faculty's commitment to excellence (and hood work ethic) results come quick and correct on whatever particular service each team is responsible for. The Love triangle despite their requiting Love for us and their craft, they've conquered their burning urge to exact revenge immediately upon learning who is responsible for crimes against us, instead they first bring their findings to the holy faculty. They have all the means and of course that infamous "Crip-Will" to avenge us however, it is their Love, Life and Loyalty for protocol and professionalism that keeps them. Noodles gathers and processes all the information through two cycles, the Strategy first then the Defense. Finally, A Nation-wide Crip faculty meeting is arranged in a suburb where civilians and local police would not notice. Faculty heads from several dominant hoods only send one Noodles representative with one Squad or Heat member (as security) as everyone is assured that the ultimate duty of security rests on the local cadre, so an escort is merely a travel formality. Our local C.S.I. takes care of all of the reconnaissance of the suburban gated community so that a member of the heat can be a mile away with a fifty caliber and day-night binoculars simply securing everyone's safety from afar. e.g. A mysterious ice cream truck approaches a block where our Faculty is in session behind closed doors or in the back yard of a location, the heat team from afar will see the truck moving closer, the benefit of the reconnaissance is to inform the heat member that no children live on this particular block so the ice cream truck is out of place. Immediate calls are made to heat and tempo members on the ground to move in closer, suddenly four kids (-3 boys and one girl) appear on bicycles playfully circling the ice cream truck just as it pulls in front of the home where our Faculty heads are inside. The driver may only see children but he is effectively being held neutralized by cannon-carrying Crips whom are ridiculously committed to excellence! These tactics are generally recommended when our faculty is meeting with hostiles or "potential" adversaries yet in circumstances where C-Nation cousins are coming in from different parts of the world, the hosting cadres are responsible for anything and everything that might in anyway threaten any Crip's personal safety and security while in our jurisdiction. Once he or she is back on transport back to their own hood we and whatever other cadrés existing along their transportation route are cleared.

The primary luxury of having Love and being Loved is the acts and the lengths that Love shows and proves for each and every one of us within the whole Nation. Only a fool would dare to test the courage of Love and especially "Our" Love!

After a successful Faculty meeting on the latest developments had concluded, things began to unfold and every team as well as other supportive cadré's all wanted to play their parts. Noodles has very carefully deliberated on a Blue printed strategy that has excellent defenses in place for reinforcement purposes reminding each team that failure is not an option. First Capital Hill negotiates a spending grant which allows them to throw a huge fundraising concert featuring various "A" list entertainers who still recognize the importance of staying mindful of the ghettos and hoods. A venue is rented, our C.S.I. assign some of their best to check and keep the tempo at a safe and secure temperature to guarantee all celebrity entertainers get nothing but "LOVE" even Crip love so they'll know they're welcome to come back. Then our Boot Camp team full of all the school age youth working towards their assignments and education are instructed to post flyers and spread the word that any issues between the races are ceased. Our C-Team being the Body and Soul is consulted and to consult with all the races (doing Incarceration time) that we wish to find resolve and end the hostilities "if" we can. The Squad is called on to open up for recruiting season and to establish a: "fists over fire arms" tone with our Local adversaries in the name of "Remembering

Manhood!". Our Tray-Com (walkway) team continues all their usual Travels and Communications routines in all their usual states except the three states where they'd been unduly put under duress. It is in these particular states where they must now coordinate with the Heat team and be fitted with bulletproof (armid fiber) clothing and carefully protected as any transaction operations proceed, so...

A modern surveillance camera rotates in a globe atop a warehouse on 640 acres of nothing, a square mile of California desert land owned by the Crips. Finally a diesel truck appears in escort fashion between two black S.U.V.s all speeding single file down a dirt road that leads to the warehouse. Immediately a Criplette inside watching her monitor yells out "in-coming! times three!" she informs "six heads deep but twelve is a likely minimum!". "I got cha'!" a heat team project manager responds, "Okay! I want six snipers up high and hot!" he barks causing urgency to fill the room as he continues "by the numbers yall lay six down with one sound on my go!".

Approximately 15 minutes later the vehicles arrive, all three dropping off an M-16 carrying gun man from their passenger side doors. Two of the men scan the perimeter while the third navigates the diesel in turning around and backing into the warehouse in their usual unloading fashion. Immediately in reciprocal normalcy the Crip's usual Tray-Com/Walkway team members open the double doors while casually greeting the travelers from Jalisco, Mexico whom they recognize and taking no particular notice of their pointed machine guns, especially not this time knowing that the Heat is in the house, tucked away in the rafters while only the Heat's project manager is on the ground and in plain sight with the Walkway team regulars. Once all six of the foreign exporters gathered at the rear of the diesel and were properly introduced to the one Crip face they weren't familiar with their inquisitive posture relaxed and finally the Crip money cases emerged. Simultaneously the diesel's big double doors swing open releasing four more gunmen who jumped out holding aim dead on all four Crips, whom had expected only to see a bed of blue agave tequilana plants. "Que pasa" our spicy Puerto Rican Criplette asked "whats up" in Spanish while her and the other three Crips are relieved of their pistols. The heat snipers up in the raptors are uneasy at the sight of all of this but disciplined enough not to squeeze as they shift their targets to prioritize who must be dropped first once the sign is given.

"Ahh, so sorry for this little surprise but you are the Crips, que no?" The Senior Mexican finally speaks up with a sinister grin "Your people have violated our Peace agreement!". He makes a hand gesture and one of the gun men goes back into the darkness of the truck's long bed and returned with two Asians and one Black-Asian. All three men are bound and gagged and have been beaten to bloody pulps.

"These men violated our Long Beach territories and must be executed" the Senior Mexican continues to explain in calm Cartel fashion "but one of my men noticed the tattoos so we decided to give you... our friends, a chance to explain and pay for their lives or watch us take their heads for you to display throughout Long Beach as a warning." An ackward silence followed for what seemed like an hour but it was barely a minute before the Senior Crip/Heat team project manager took a step forward "Having tattoos don't make these folks no Crips" he explains calmly "let them speak and identify themselves to us, then we will determine if they are one of us". The Senior Mexican nods and his men remove the gags from the three battered men. Immediately one of them blurts out "Hey Cuz, we're Crips and I'll explain" "-Hold up cousin!" Our Cuban Crip raises his hand gesturing the Asian speaker to slow down then he asks: "Are y'all C-Nation?" they nod yes in unison with confident yes gestures. "Well, let us hear the Pledge!" our Criplette blurts out insistently causing the three men to respond:

"I pledge allegiance to the blue flag and the Consolidated Crip Nation,

Whether behind bars or in Public, which through both we must stand,
One Nation, under God, Indivisible, with liberty, pushing love, life and loyalty for All."

Silence falls over the room like a blanket but is quickly lifted as one of the Mexican, gunmen gets locked into a stare down with one of the battered Crips that completed the pledge. "Hey! Que Pasa? You piece of shit, look forward!" the gunner kicks the Crip in the back, telling him to continue facing everybody else's way instead of peering backwards over his shoulder.

"Easy! Easy!" The Senior Crip of the heat speaks soothingly "just one more thing..." he asks the Senior Mexican who nods for him to proceed with his probe. "Can y'all recite the Oath?" he asks the three bound men ever so cautiously. The moment suddenly became tense for all the Crips in the room and in the rafters because nobody can hear the oath uttered before he or she has been screened and blessed by a bona fide Crip. "No!" One of the bound men answered angrily only to be kicked in the back by another gunner standing behind him. "Listen to me cousins..." the Sr. Heat project manager begins "Protocol will be protected, I know this seems inappropriate but trust me, you won't be in violation!"

The three Crips look at each other, not knowing if this was a test of the true identities or if it was a test of their adherence to Crip protocol, they decided to trust his words:

In a slow Methodical chant-like synchronization the men all spoke these words:

If ever I should break from the norm and not stay true to form
If ever I fail to honor the Land and loving my Criplettes and Crip man
If ever I abandon a Crip's side and not represent with Crip pride
Do or die, Revenge is an art, a thousand deaths, cut out my heart
Cremate my body if I'm a liar, dispose the ashes but savour the fire!
If ever I'm not standing tall, through it all, like a brick wall, refusing to fall
If ever I should fail to take a stand against knife, gun or hand to hand
Forever a Crip shall fear no man, Death before dishonor, this I understand!

Suddenly the heat's project manager snorted in deeply, then loudly summoned a lugi up from the back of his throat and finally with a little tilt of his head to the left he spit to the ground but before the lugi could hit the dirt, one loud explosion erupted from up above everyone's heads and immediately six of the most alert looking gunmen fell dead, their skulls appearing like bursted watermelons. The second and third round of gunfire (being orchestrated by the three prong spit signal) still sounded precise and final as the remaining gunmen barely had time to properly assess the situation before they were being flipped backwards and forward into eternal sleep. Instantly the heat and their project manager descended on the truck's cab and the S.U.V.'s out front to clean up all that remained of this would-be Cartel Kill squad while the Walkway Crips untied the three cousins that had been abducted and scheduled for execution and their heads publicized as a symbolic display of power. No Crip shall ever allow the execution of another by the hands of any outsider, however... Crips do discipline their own and these three had alot of questions to answer, alot of explaining to do for these tensions they have caused between us and our Blue Agave Tequilana plant suppliers.

The TRG cousins had grown in size considerably and obviously was occupying a much larger portion of Long Beach than that which was initially claimed and agreed upon. Subsequently they had also had a few local skirmishes with the Long Beach Crips leading to an unofficial rift that led them to believe they would have only been an unnecessary distraction if they had attended the latest, most recent Nation meeting. Ultimately, it was still determined that the Mexicans had spilled first blood instead of using the treaty agreement to make their grievances known. There was still something sinister underlying the Mexicans hate for us despite the fact that we're up against the same poverty obstacles as they are and so, to move forward we might just have to respectfully move on without them.

Due in large part to the Excellence of the Tray-Com teams Nation wide and our faculty members and architects who designed this whole strategy and its defense on an international scale, we tapped into more honorable suppliers in Columbia and Panama to operate with in case the Mexicans dislike for us became an issue. Peace is almost always what results when powerful enterprises value "Honor" and "Respect" over their own egos and pride. In big business, Peace provides for Prosperity and only the lack of "Honor" and/or "Respect" leads an enterprise into exaggerated visions of grandeur so that they begin to underestimate their own consortium partners. Nevertheless our Tray-Com team are masters of travelings and Communications and their job is to always, always have secure "Walkways" for the cadre to depend on.

Old walkways and old bridges can be rebuilt in the event that a transgressor has come to some sort of realizations but trust will have to be earned, as we don't look to furnish nobody with fresh opportunities to try to even some type of score. Crips shall never lose in a tit-for-tat war yet we see no benefit in being locked in a life-long war campaign because we already have plenty of those and they don't at all yield the lucrative returns befitting such a Nation as ours.

It is true for us that to whom much is given, much more is required, no matter how big or how small each tribe or community may be. All Crips as a Consolidated Crip Nation are duty bound to be high-minded and farther thinking than most civilian mortals are. We must understand and then overstand the importance of legacy above and beyond whatever broad expressions might currently rule the day. Our form and function must be like water even exactly like water. Our motions and movements must be fluid at times then frozen still at other times. We must possess and maintain an heir of indestructibility under pressure just as certain as the water in pipes and hydrants remain relentless, unable to be broken or crushed under the most enormous pressures that the pipes and hydrants can stand. Our destinations and determinations must be deliberate like the rivers and streams which so stubbornly carve their own pathway through mountains, deserts and rocky roads proving their unwillingness to being detoured or denied. With these H2O characteristics that we have absorbed, we master the art of reformulation and reform so that just like water faced with the omnipotent powers of fire we blessedly can survive by becoming heavy vapors and gases seeking cooler temperatures to reconvene in or when faced with the heart-stopping, life-stopping powers of the freezing cold we simply turn into a solid holding still as ice. We are fashioned to endure any and every challenge that this existence has to offer, so it's no wonder why in times of war we come down on our adversaries like a heavy rain making it so inevitable that they are gonna get wet. We are the Consolidated Crip Nation and through these nine holy disciplines of our Crip Faculty we become immortal. Can't stop won't stop until the last drip drops!!!

In this whole particular instance our Holy Faculty was compelled to facilitate Justice for aprx. three lost souls and their families as Noodles and C.S.I. had promised. The beautiful girl whose young body was mutilated and discarded in a heap of flames like trash against the sidewalk. Her death was the tipping point because she was directly related to blue blood, but also the other two youth were of equal importance to the process and final outcome. Our Communities must be able to depend on us absolutely and we must be dependable absolutely, even excellently! Most Communities would much rather call the Crips over calling the cops because they know and can sense that only one of the two is genuinely committed to love, live for and die for particular communities (for free) while the other is paid in 8 hr. shifts and still just barely tolerates it upon each corner they turn, terrorizingly issuing ticket after ticket. No other country out right declares war on its own communities (who pay into their government worker's salaries-via-taxes) accept in America. The truth is: the war on crime, war on gangs, war on drugs, war on poverty and any other word compounded with war as a government action is wrong because war is war by any name and no community within a Capitalistic setting deserves such policies being visited upon it. Any war coupled with Capitalism can only produce profit and self righteousness on one side and poverty with despondency and criminalized desperation on the other side. This actuality occurring all across America is stoically accepted and politicized as: "The Justice System: So, For the more elite communities within the C-Nation we can no longer engage in the open-ended, on-going Chaotic wars we once favored because history has shown us that only our own community loses. Peace is almost always what results when powerful enterprises value "Respect" and "Integrity" (which is the adherence to a code of values). It is only the lack of one of these which then produces those heavy, heavy illusions of grandeur and inspires underestimations between those enterprises and ultimately schemes, plots and misunderstandings bring about detrimental business and war miscalculations.

The Crip Nation has evolved and because we believe that our show of integrity trumps our show of brute power; when our Texas cadré acquired two hundred kilos from the very same Cartel through a similar warehouse engagement together we devised a plan to promote, resolve & before the end of the day our consorts in Columbia and Peru have communicated to the Mexican leader that his money is still "his" as was agreed upon pursuant to our contract and that the Crips only came for the souls we felt were debted to us by his hand. Finally a wire account number was provided and our business was concluded. Integrity trumps power!

"One who knows the enemy and himself will not be endangered in 100 engagements... One who does not know the enemy but knows himself will sometimes be victorious and will sometimes meet with defeat... One who knows neither the enemy nor himself will invariably be defeated in every engagement!"   - Niccolo Machiavelli

Integrity trumps power! This Holy faculty is our legitimate means for making our lives and everyones lives more positive and productive.

Knowing ourselves means: we don't rob our own resources nor do we crush our own communities and we do not abuse the facilities that we use. This Holy facilitation is merely one example, not just about exacting revenge but about impacting the existences and co-existences of the Nation, of each Cadré, of our communities and our consorts into a healthy cohesive functioning underworld which allows us to turn our own streets and homes into the upper-class expensive communities we are gated out of, all while still pursuing our own designs for prosperity. Use this Faculty and choose this faculty to use you so that you'll never lose again. Eastside, Westside, Northside, Southside, Nation wide, Unified: Community Raised Infantry Progressing! Chin up, Chest out this is what its all about! Facilitating Love, Life, and Loyalty Excellently.

"READ THE BIBLE TO BE WISE" BELIEVE
THE BIBLE TO BE SAFE...
PRACTICE IT TO BE HOLY!!!"

VIII. The Kiwe Dog

The PitBull Dog

[[insert picture 01 here]]

Our soul's reincarnation, it was slain in frustration,

Our reborn manifestation, returns to serve the C-Nation,

In the form of a dog with the swag of a Hog the Pitbull fuccs your imagination!!!

The Courts deem her the worst, new laws to put her in a hearse,

allowing cops to shoot first, they all blame her for her thirst,

In the form of a dog with the swag of a Hog the Pitbull is a Crip not a curse!!!

Never let it be said, a hood Pitbull likes red,

Cuz the only blood she bled, was on fighting the meat she's fed,

In the form of a dog with the swag of a Hog the Pitbull is the Truth, Crip bred!!!

On January 17th, 1969 a venerated Alprentice "Bunchy" Carter and Jon Huggins were just two Community Revolutionaries In Progress for the advancement of their Los Angeles chapter of the Black Panther Party when on this day they were cut down leaving behind a cloud of gun smoke and lingering frustrations that such promise and potential was silenced on the U.C.L.A. campus at Campbell Hall. Yet as the echoes from the gun blasts faded into nothingness those ride or die souls of theirs just weren't ready to surrender and disappear. Likewise when the venerated Raymond Washington and that young, proud and pregnant Donnesha Ray Rider was taken from us just as the fertile royal blue rose of solidarity began to blossom from the concrete soil of the underworld communities, it was their spirited souls that 1st chanted: "Crips don't die, we multiply!" in their last mortal breaths and so they did, causing the first Pitbull dogs to be born in a litter of six: (3-boys, 3-girls) in a ghetto alley under an abandoned old chevy. Just like many of us even today, their arrival was met with no media buz, no concern for how they'd live or eat, no records of their parents or exactly what cross bred miracle or mixture designed such a pure dog however, there are many myths, assessments and biological assumptions that high society finally concocted to satisfy their own egos so that it seems they are completely aware and concerned. They know all and can easily explain all the dynamics and genetics that created us and our dog but really... they don't know! They don't know like we know, they don't know like these Holy Crip Scriptures know, they don't know like the streets and hoods know and therefore basically...they don't know!

If truth be told, the whole species of dog evolved from the wolf packs located closest to human tribes and Neanderthal staging areas where they could easily become scavengers instead of predators. Certain breeds of wolf became dependant on trash and scraps so much that their K-9's and head structure shrank considerably. A quani m leap experiment took place at Belyaev where the less aggressive wolf pups were separated and continuously cross bred with each other until finally a docile set of fluffy eared wolves with fluffy black and white coats resembling a common dog emerged.

Our knowledge of having this direct (reincarnated) cousin called the Pitbull came to us in a much more dynamic fashion. The revelation of the Pitbull was Gangster!

A fragile old man hobbled slowly into the Los Angeles County jail's Crip module, one of the most violent confinements in the world (at the time) where living depended absolutely on how willing you were to die.

This old man claimed no particular hood and the only tattoo every one noticed right away was just four numbers on his forehead: "3•18•9•16". He said his name was god-gib and although we found it strange and different, most of us had heard of or personally had stranger names ourselves so "god-gib" it was. He spoke in a raspy, low tone which normally would not have been heard over the usual raucous our Crip module was known for on a daily basis yet, on this day we all heard him and we All listened...

"Esteemed Greetings Cuzzins, it's an honor and a privilege for me to be here amongst you all" his voice was calm and measured yet it still managed to create a paralyzing echo that captured all the ears of Abel row, Baker row, Denver row and Charlie row where he spoke from. He told us he once headed the biggest dog pound in the State and that in the wee hours he would listen to the dogs talking to one another. Many of us let out a brief laugh, and although I couldn't see the old man I felt eerily certain that he wasn't laughing with us, he was dead serious. His facility had 15 different rows of cages he explained, each row had 30 cages which each held one dog, (remarkably similar to the state of the art Pelican-Bay Security Housing units of modern times) and of his 450 dogs 250 were Chihuahuas, 150 were German Shepherds, 30 were Pitbulls, 10 were Akitas and 10 were common mutts. Immediately voices throughout the module began mumbling at their nearest homie: "aw cuz, I had a down ass Pit!", "Cuz, you know I had a blue Pit!", "Oh yea... I had a red nose" etc... "You Pitbulls are stupid as fucc!" the old mans raspy voice cut through the nostalgic moment we were all caught up in as he continued unapologetically "You Pitbulls are your own worst enemy!" "Hey!, Hey! Hold up Pop!" One Crip's disapproving voice from Baker row sounded off followed by another from Abel now "Yea godgib or whatever the fucc your name is... you bettá kickback on that disrespect to the Pitbull!", "Yea, you know?" "Hey Young Cousins, I'm telling the story right?, this is the shit the Chihuahuas were all saying to the Pitbulls down at my place" the old man explained and the utter silence after he spoke invited him to continue the story, "the Pitbull fight and bite so they are kept far from one another and the Chihuahuas would get together every night after lights out and just ridicule the Pitbull for all its faults and all the disadvantages it brings on itself for being so mean and unpredictable to humans. "You dumb ass Pitbulls don't bark enough to be the type of guard dog that folks are all looking for" one Chihuahua pointed out as a German Shepherd chimed in "Yea, and You Pitbulls aren't willing to be trained like we are… humans love us for our loyalty!" All this ridicule and laughter prodded the Pitbull every day and night as he'd pace in his cage silently after hearing their criticisms which were pretty close to always true. "Hey yall," the Akita with an Asian accent called out to all the Chihuahua's and German Shepherds, "do yall remember the time they tried to bring two of those Pitbull clowns together?" suddenly all the dogs roared in laughter as the Akita continued, "they chewed through their cage mesh to try to kill each other! Ha! Ha! Ha! Yep!". Finally the Pitbull was tired of hearing them mocking his nature so he finally spoke out to defend himself. "I'm a muthafuccin gangster, I'm a rider, I'm a natural born killer and y'all fools can't see me or be me so y'all hate on me but I am what I am!" the Pitbull circled his tiny cage and then lay his huge heavy head down a chewed up food dish which he'd just destroyed earlier in the day (just as he does every day when they provide him a new one). Meanwhile a dog pound employee who routinely makes his rounds to check on all the dogs arrived with a pouch full of his off-the-record-dog treats which as always he tossed into all the German Shepherds and a few selected Chihuahuas, Akitas and even a mutt or two. These treats are to inspire their best behavior and discipline within the ranks of each dog's group-dynamic. However, as always, the Pitbull was never worthy of such treats, he is never cooperative and the Pitbulls have no group unity therefore no consensus-good behavior can ever be inspired by one being treated kindly or remotely fair. To the dog keepers, the Pitbull seems to be perfectly content with having a hard life, being denied and despised somehow perfectly made the Pitbull's day. After the keeper left the dog tiers, the Chihuahuas began to talk in Spanish, look pityingly upon the Pitbull laying all alone beside his chewed up bowl then they'd smile and laugh until they fell asleep for the night. The German Shepherd and the Akitas and the mutts all conversed with their own kind, laughed and enjoyed each other's company in their own perspective languages while mumbling how stupid Pitbulls are. The Pitbull knows to himself and herself that they are not stupid and if opportunity and occasion ever happens to meet so that their cages ever opened the Pitbull would gladly teach these "intelligent" dogs how to do the deadly Pitbull shake and shuffle dance, ya' dig?" Ha! Ha! Ha! smile! Laughter ping ponged off the

Crip module walls as godgib concluded the story. Although it didn't seem to have a point or a solution we all felt it to our core where it hurt and felt good at the same time.

Early the next morning before breakfast I struck up a kite to slide to godgib about how I appreciated the stories he sent us to bed with, when, as I wrote his name it seemed so familiar to me. I know I'd never known anyone by this name yet it was like I'd known and written this name down many times before and finally it hit me... "Big Dog" was this man's true handle. I couldn't contain myself, I yelled over the tier to Charlie row "Njema Asa bui Kiwes!" (Good morning Crips) this allows me to use the tier without over riding anyones convo "Hey Big Dog!" I yelled "Yea godgib I got you Ha! Ha! Ha!" I laughed as others began to have the same light bulb moment. "Aw cuz, he's gone!" someone from Charlie row yelled to all of us calling him. It became a huge mystery because according to the staff and all the transfer records, no one had ever moved into the Crip module or into that cell on yesterday. The guards assumed we were up to our antics of course, We knew better... Finally in the midst of all the commotion we returned from breakfast chanting the four numbers on the old man's forehead. Numbers we should have instantly recognized. C-3, R-18, I-9, P-16. The old man godgib (Big Dog) had the alphabetic equivalent for Crip in numbers tattooed on his forehead. And his messege was solely regarding... Tha' Dog!

Now, in real talk we all know society has tried to capture and control everything that is us and mimic our Royal Swag in everything so of course our dog is now as much a world wide sensation as we are, however they don't know...They don't know that the Crip dog is not a toy dog, a house pooch or a weeny dog. The Pitbull is one of us and he's been here before so perhaps he or she can finally forgive civilians of their disdain for us but I doubt he'll ever forget. This sadly becomes clear when a Pitbull has its flashback and kills the child carelessly hitting him with the plastic toy bat. Countless episodes of viciousness has been reported on by the media trying to demonize this dog but the Pitbull remains unfazed. He/she knows the biz... loved by few, hated by many, respected by all! The Pitbull knew their love (his/her civilian custodians) came with conditions so save the crocodile tears when you've authorized the veterinarian to "Put her down!" or "Put'em to sleep!" because the Pitbull already knew your true colors werent the same royal hue as ours so Love, Life and Loyalty means nothing at all once he's shaken to death your child. But... as for us, we remain committed, even then, no matter what. As our C-dog is committed to us, never to civilians. Note: This dog is capable of barking but he or she remains uninterested in living the life of a snitch. Her nose can smell for drugs or cadavers but she insists that her soul wasnt reincarnated to become no pig or officer McGruff riding in the back seat of a K-9 patrol car. This C-dog is capable of seeing but he/she remains uninterested in being a civilian guide dog or helping old ladies cross the street. The Pitbull has heard the pitch and all the perks from the German Shepherd who said the pay is good yet this dog is thirsty for more. You must not insult the C-dog by expecting her to go fetch the newspaper or your house slippers, the machinery that is her jaw bone is designed for mass destruction and crushing of bones, locking on loose skin and shaking her victim to pieces. The C-dog has knowledge of the call of the wild but has zero interests in pulling no sleds through the snow. The Pitbull ain't interested in herding civilians sheeps or cows and Crips aint about to be chasing no foxes or collecting the fowl you've shot out the sky. Our reincarnated loved one has returned for business and that's why her interest is usually regarding death and violence. It has been recently discovered that dogs can sense and even smell approval vibes from its handler and perhaps trains his or herself to act out in concert with what might make that handler happy. Well... we've observed this for decades as we would patrol our neighborhoods with our Pitbull pulling fiercely at the chains and weights we've got her on then all of a sudden she notices a mutt across the street and signal to us to cut her loose on it. But just like black folks who'd do anything to please their handlers, sometimes the flaw is not in the dog but in the handler himself. Some handlers enjoy turning their Pit into a pet, exactly the way some black folks are turned into loyal pets. The handler disgraces him or her by training them to fetch Frisbees and house slippers and convince a predator Pitbull that he's a retriever dog, a police guard dog or any number of fabricated identities just because of where they and their handler are located. Suddenly a Pitbull raised on a farm will fight to death proving he/she is a herding dog. This docile personality is evidenced from human culture where black folks world wide deny their flesh blackness and fight tooth and nail to proclaim they are bi-racial, mixed, they're Dominican, or Cuban, Belizean, Columbian, Brazilian, Egyptian, Puerto Rican or British, etc... So, as Crip handlers, we must allow the Pitbull to be who he or she actually is and to do whatever he/she was reincarnated to do as it is our duty to raise them "true to form."

#1. Pitbull pups shall not be overly handled (cuddled with human hands) but lightly slapped and popped on their nose until they develop the keen sense to snap at any hand approaching their face.

#2. Pitbulls must be taunted with towels and tug of war battles which will allow it thoroughly to hone in on its locking and shaking skills. These tug of wars must begin in their early puppy years and carry on into adulthood where a Pitbull can actually be even lifted off its feet or swung around in the air (carefully) from refusing to release his end of the beach towel.

#3. The Pitbull must always be burdened with a heavy weight/yoke around his or her neck as you both go for long walks and runs. This process starts light when the Pit is a pup but must constantly increase as her neck and legs adapt and develop naturally as the months and years pass. The reality about toughness is that it only comes through the enduring of tough-times and tough circumstances... all tough guys know that! When our yoke is removed, its no wonder we walk so proud and tall, its no wonder that when the Pitbull's weight is taken off, once his yoke is removed, his fight is so strong and even effortless as he handles the weight of his foe like a rag doll and the outcome is usually pretty ugly for the other dog. Ghetto toughness is not easily defeated which is why we as Crips perform so aggressively and much like the Pitbull we effortlessly can handle the weight of our foes and again the outcome is usually pretty ugly for the other individuals.

#4. The Pitbull should periodically be fed raw meat that strengthens his powerful jaw muscles as well as keeps him acquainted with flesh and thirsty for blood. Some of us have mythical feeding methods that make our Pitbulls meaner and consensus was unable to choose just one so... with Love, Life, and Loyalty as your moral compass and "do no harm" as your conscious intention you choose what safely toughens up your Pitbull: Hot chili peppers, jalapenos stuffed in beef then denying him or her any water for 30 minutes is one widely used method. Gun powder sprinkled on steak meat is another method, 3 days with water and no food then beer & bones on the 3rd day is yet another method and it all seems cruel from a civilians perspective but... they don't know! The cruelty we've all endured and what our Pit endures is what builds and also reveals the character which is uniquely ours alone but they don't know...!

#5. The Pitbull should be thoroughly groomed in true Crip fashion which is a fighting fashion. This means he/she should not be burdened with unnecessary extremities for his foe to lock on to (e.g. a long tail or long ears). The Pitbull's nails should be appropriately trimmed so that they are strong and not at risk to break off too deeply in the event of a fight on the pavement.

#6. The Pitbull must be worked out regularly and not just physically but also psychologically, this means that he or she (just like many of us) absolutely needs to earn & feel your pride and approval. Your pride and approval at his/her performance on a battlefield. In short, you've gotta' give your Pitbull some fights! A few exhibition fights to allow your Pit to feel how superior he/she is to another dog that has had no rigorous conditioning. This not only builds confidence but it also allows you and your Pitbull to bond on a psychological level with emotional and spiritual proclivities as well.

#7. The Pitbull must also be provided with a balance of professionalism. This means that we can run a toughy-diet on him or her only once in a while and after he or she proves its blue-steel to the core, stop it! Balance of professionalism means we abide by the scriptures and balance in the book knowledge and studies of the day which might benefit our Pitbull. Balance of professionalism towards the Kiwe dog is a duty we respect under the code of Love, Life and Loyalty with our commitment to our own excellence. Nobody shall adore the Pitbull as much as we do. Bow wow yippy yo' yippy yay!

IX. About The Crips

This sacred book is not about sex, violence, money and murder as folks might assume, this is a holy text "about the Community Raised Infantry Progressing." These Scriptures are about and for a regular people who'd never be able to afford or qualify to attend the prestigious Ivy League colleges despite deserving and needing them more! This, the Holy Crip's Bible is about Love, its about Life and its about Loyalty all put into motion to make the hopeless communities hopeful, to make the degenerate conditions and social climates more honorable and fertile for positive growth and most importantly, it's to do all of this excellently! In a world full of the shrewdest misconceptions and deliberate deceptions "about the Crips". We've been aware of the hyperbolic political themes and media-driven inferences "about the Crips", we feel-to-death the draconian laws and sinister Judge opinions "about the Crips", the hateful peace officer unions and furious victim's groups of folks we have never victimized "about the Crips", the U.S. postage and prison vendor price hikes "about the Crips" and still there's so much more "about the Crips!"

Theres Blue Magic and Blue Steel... Blue Kush and the Blue Pill "about the Crips"! The Blue allegiances and Blue Print C-D's... Blue Ivy Love and Blue blooded G-Ds "about the Crips"! That Blue Lambo with the Blue rims, the true blue goons in their blue Timb's "about the Crips"! Sexy Blue hair and nails, electric blue eyes...Blue silk panties under all blue skies "about the Crips"! and even through it all, the good and the bad, the highs and the lows, one thing is for sure and its the one thing Everybody knows "about the Crips", from the cradle to the grave, You just can't stop the Crips!!!

THE TEN COMMANDMENTS

1. Thou Shall Not Snitch, Imply, or Inform in cooperation with Authorities.
2. Thou Shall Not Rape, Molest or Engage in Male Homosexual Behavior.
3. Thou Shall Fear No Man, Turn Down or Run Out from a fight or a D.P.
4. Thou Shall Not Kill No Man, Woman or Animal of the 'Royal' Cloth. (Per Due Process)
5. Thou Shall Not Hate on Our own nor take part in racial hate crimes.
6. Thou Shall Not Dishonor, Disrespect or Slander The Crip Meritocracy.
7. Thou Shall Not Produce no type of weapon in response to a fair fight or a D.P.
8. Thou Shall Not Abandon a fallen (or Incarcerated) Crip Soul in Need.
9. Thou Shall Display Excellence, Integrity and Sobriety in All Matters Deemed Serious.
10. Thou Shall Always & Forever Honor thy God, The Laws, Thy Love, Thy Life & Thy Loyalty.

THESE COMMANDMENTS SHALL NOT CE'BROKEN!

Eastside-Westside-Northside-Southside-Nationwide-Unified!

Raymond & Reggie Washington, Tookie & Jimel, James Miller, Bunchy & Ken Carter, Blue The Two "Famous" Architects, Mike & Den Johnson, Concepcion, Barefoot Pookie, Big Dog, Craig & Tony Craddock, Roc, Buck, The Day Family, The Hub & The Dub "Hitters", BJ & Hash, Harlems Big Bob, Tim, Chili, Tike, Wattt, Lil Bit, Lil Bo, Al Capone, Poochie, Forehead Doc, Frosty, Earthquake, Looney, Smiley, Grego, N-Dog, Reece, Frog, Crip Toe, Keda, Six-Owe Motor Mouse, Mel Roc, Big Buff, Big U, Bandit, Sleep Roc, Peanut, C-Rob, K-Roc, Brynhurst, Finest, Poppa T, Lil Rip, C-Rag, Polo, Swanto, Lil Diamond, Flintstone, Rabbit, Tiny BooBoo, East Coast J-Box, LaLa, C' Dave, Doc Thone, Snoopy Blue, Q-ric, Sad, Lil Man, Mont & Greedy, 8 Tray's Big Diamond, Crazy D, Stag, Mad Bone, Tooks, Pup, Timmy Tucker, Spike, Country, My lil Bro's amd cuzins,: U.G-Droop, Harlem Sosa, Bleu Evyl, Creeper, Pop Nose, Baby Kato

From the Gutter to the Dirt, From Oceanside to San Diego, From Denver HMC to the whole East Coast.

<u>The Golden Rule</u>: ***"Everything To The Left Cuz The System Ain't Right!"***

About the Author

A true native of South Central Los Angeles, born and bred. The eldest of four boys, (one adopted -via- ghetto protocols) the author's Mother, Rev. Sister Phillips being and educator, most summers were reserved for road trips across the U.S.A. Travels of a man-child particularly to the slums and lower bottoms of each state between California to D.C. and from the Golden State to Canada.

The author became the king of the classroom in the 1st and 2nd grade at Baldwin Hills Elementary while living in a nearby housing project. 3rd grade was spent in Altadena's own Audubon Elementary until fighting returned him to Worthington Elementary for the 4th grade then Manchester Elementary for the 5th and 6th grade where fighting won him the title: "King of the School", 7th grade was cut in half between Bret Harte Preparatory Middle School to a new system called Westside Alternative. (One of only four Alternative Schools in Los Angeles) where he managed until the 1st half of the 9th grade. Then the second half at the prestigious Westchester High School where by the middle of the 10th grade fighting landed him in a squad car on the way to juvenile hall.

L.A.'s roughest continuation schools (under Tri-C) became the order of the day. Chevrot Hills B.K.A. Hamilton High Continuation, Walt Whitman B.K.A. Fairfax High Continuation, Daniel Freeman Occupational Center B.K.A. Central Adult High School, Downtown Continuation B.K.A. Metro Continuation, and C.Y.S.A.F. or Community Youth Sports/Arts Foundation.

Finally a slew of state youth and adult facilities, multiple max. and super-max. prison's, isolation units, segregated housings and then

California's infamous "end of the line" Pelican Bay. Short Corridor - S.H.U. Being a product of constant Church pews while paying all ghetto dues made me.

A combination of vast ghetto experiences throughout America and incarcerations throughout California and Las Vegas, Nevada informs the author not in a way that makes him an author but in that way that makes him a credible truth teller. Summa Cum Laude of the Underworld.

— Kiwe Don Phillips

www.ingramcontent.com/pod-product-compliance
Lightning Source LLC
Chambersburg PA
CBHW051450250726
48655CB00001B/332